Paul Simon *for* Easy Piano

Photo by Warner Brothers / Photofest

ISBN 978-1-61780-681-0

EXCLUSIVELY DISTRIBUTED BY

7777 W. BLUEMOUND RD. P.O. BOX 13819 MILWAUKEE, WI 53213

Visit Hal Leonard Online at
www.halleonard.com

AMERICAN TUNE

Words and Music by
PAUL SIMON

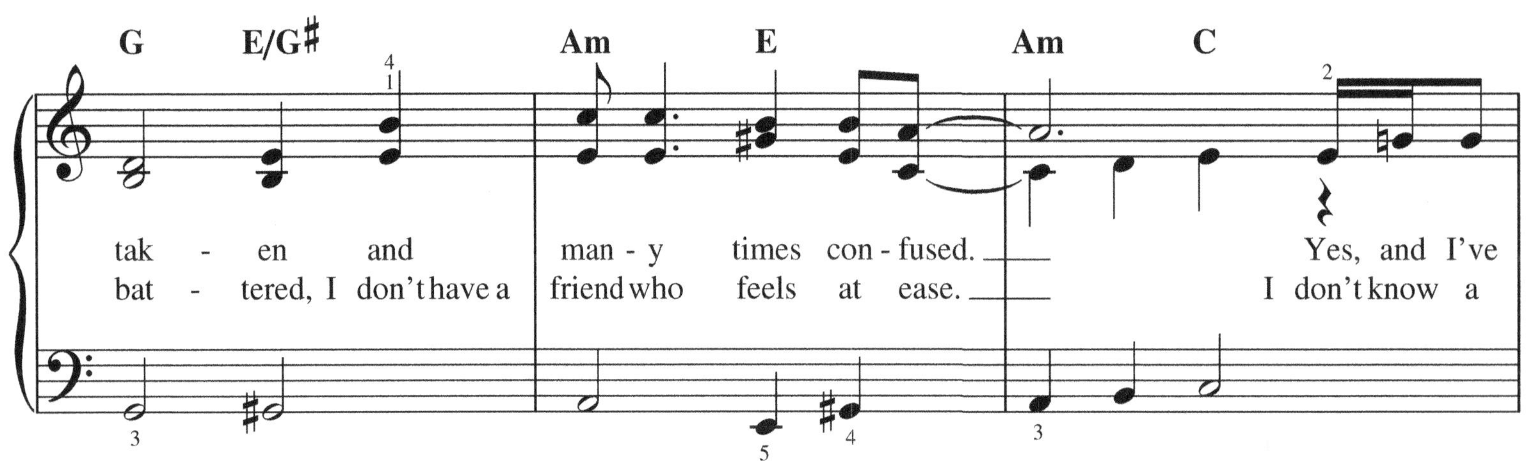

Am C7 F G F C
Oh, but I'm al - right, I'm al - right, I'm just
Oh, but it's al - right, it's al - right, for we
F C/E G G♯dim7 Am A7 D7 G
To Coda
weary to my bones. Still, you don't ex - pect to be
lived so well so long. Still, when I think of the
C G D G C F C/E G
bright and bon - vi - vant so far a - way from home,
road we're trav - 'lin on, I won - der what's gone wrong,
1.
E Am Dm7 C/G G C
so far a-way from home. I don't know a

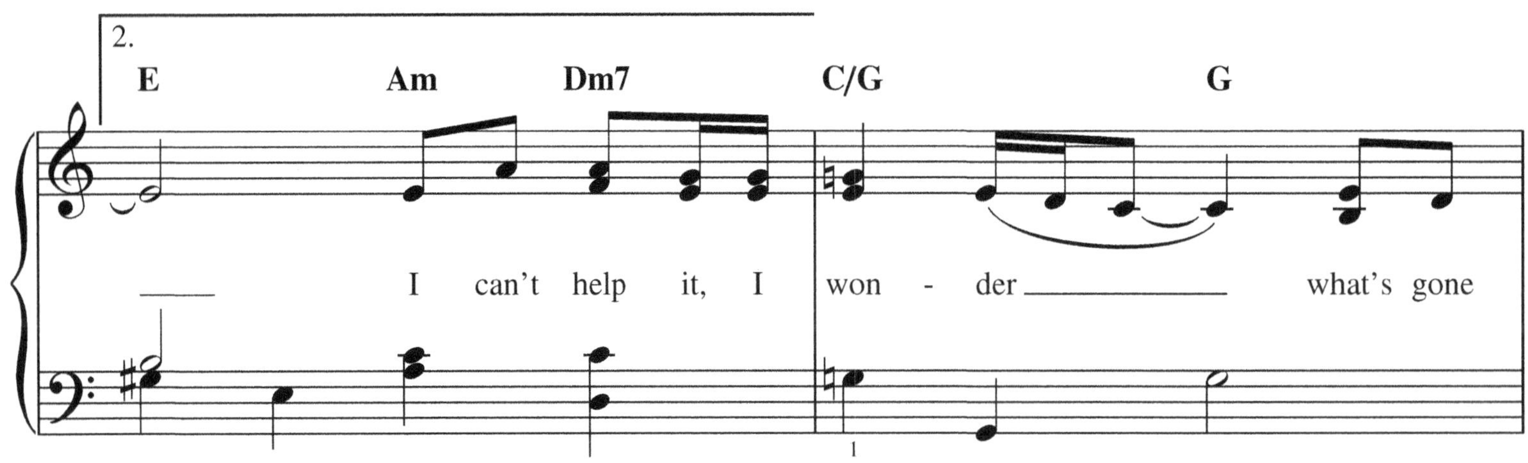
2.
E
Am
Dm7
C/G
G
I can't help it, I won - der what's gone

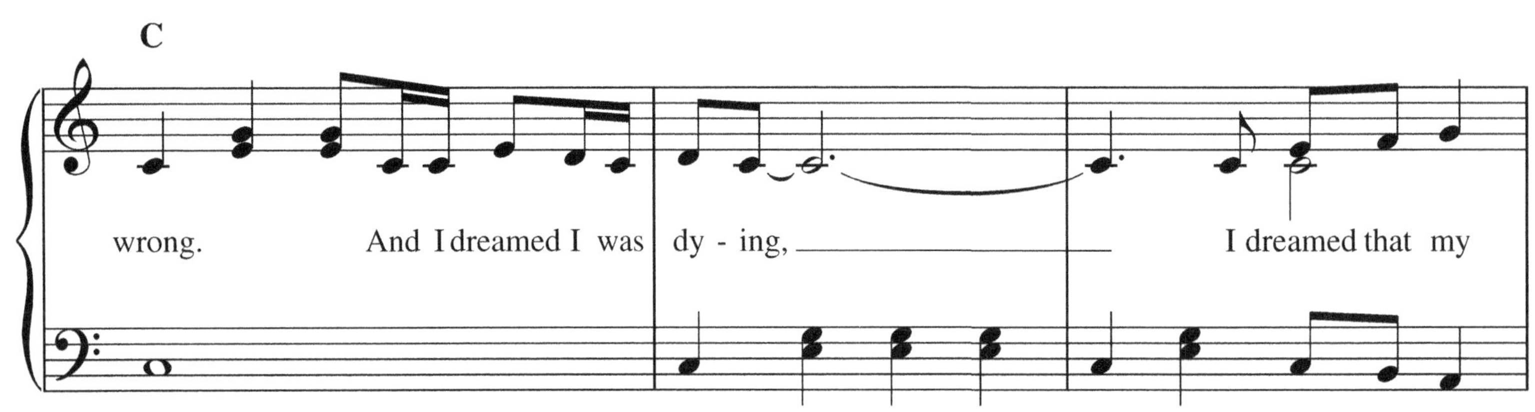
C
wrong. And I dreamed I was dy - ing,
I dreamed that my

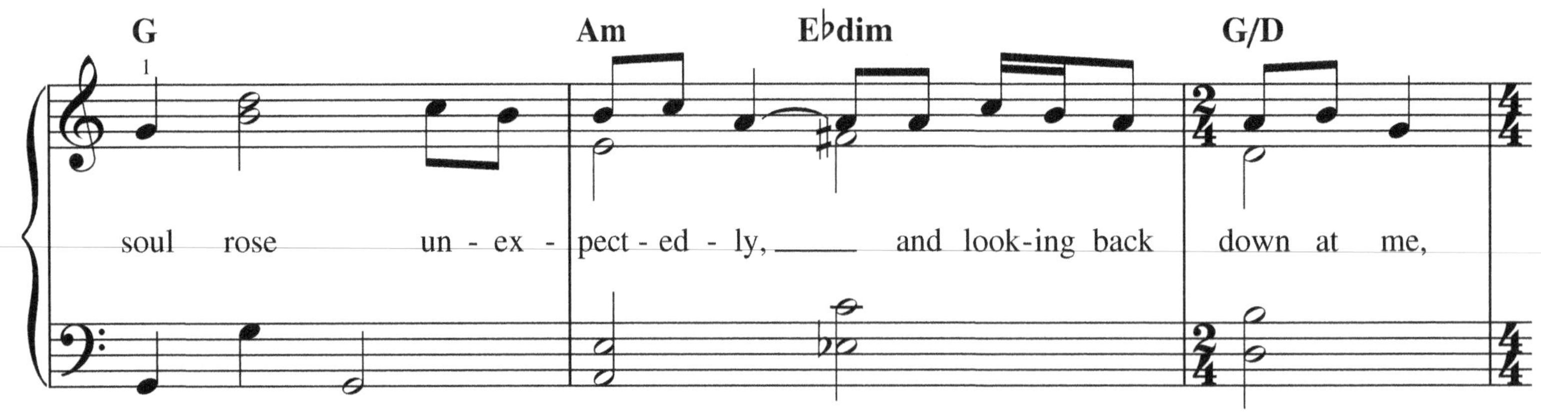
G
Am
E♭dim
G/D
soul rose un - ex - pect - ed - ly, and look-ing back down at me,

F
C
G/B
G
C
smiled re-as-sur-ing-ly. And I dreamed I was fly - ing,

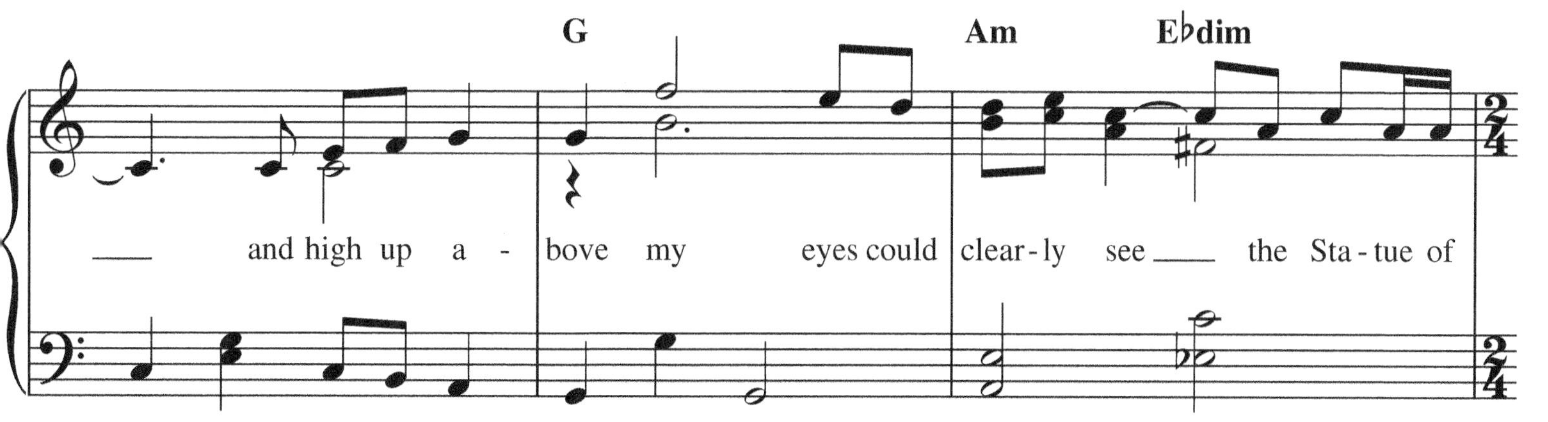
G
Am
E♭dim
and high up a - bove my eyes could clear-ly see the Sta-tue of

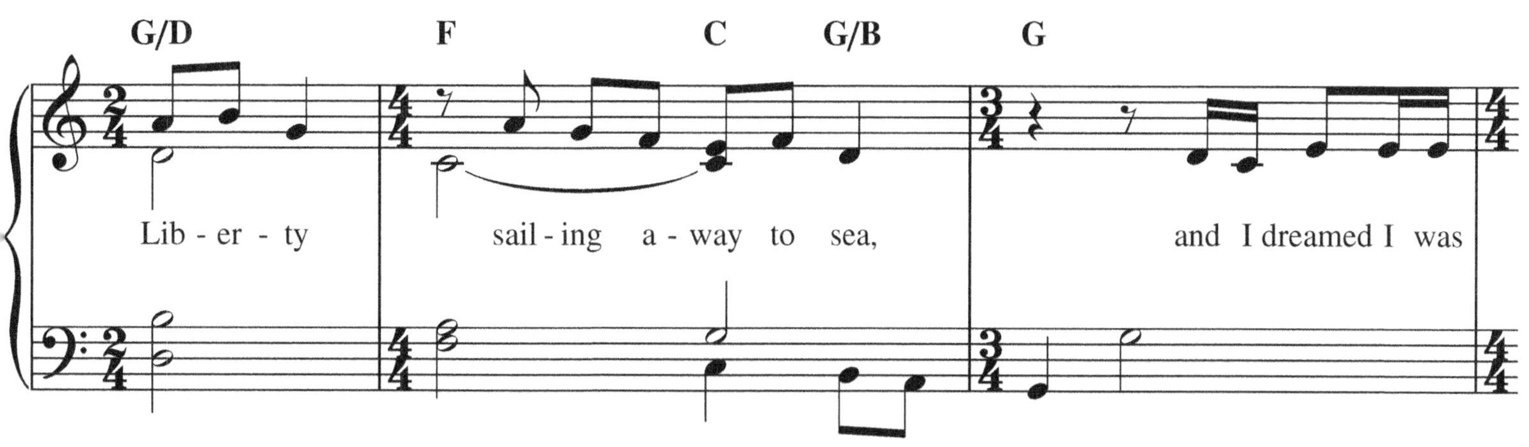
G/D
F
C
G/B
G
Lib - er - ty sail - ing a - way to sea, and I dreamed I was

C
D.S. al Coda
fly - ing. We come on the

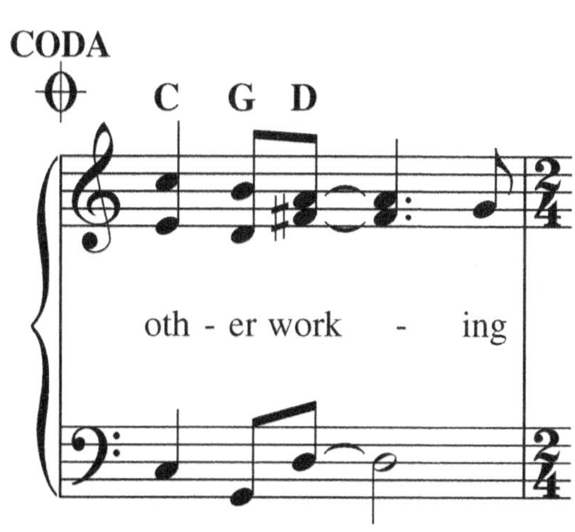
CODA
C G D
oth - er work - ing

G C
F C/E G E
Am Dm
day, and I'm try - ing to get some rest. That's all I'm

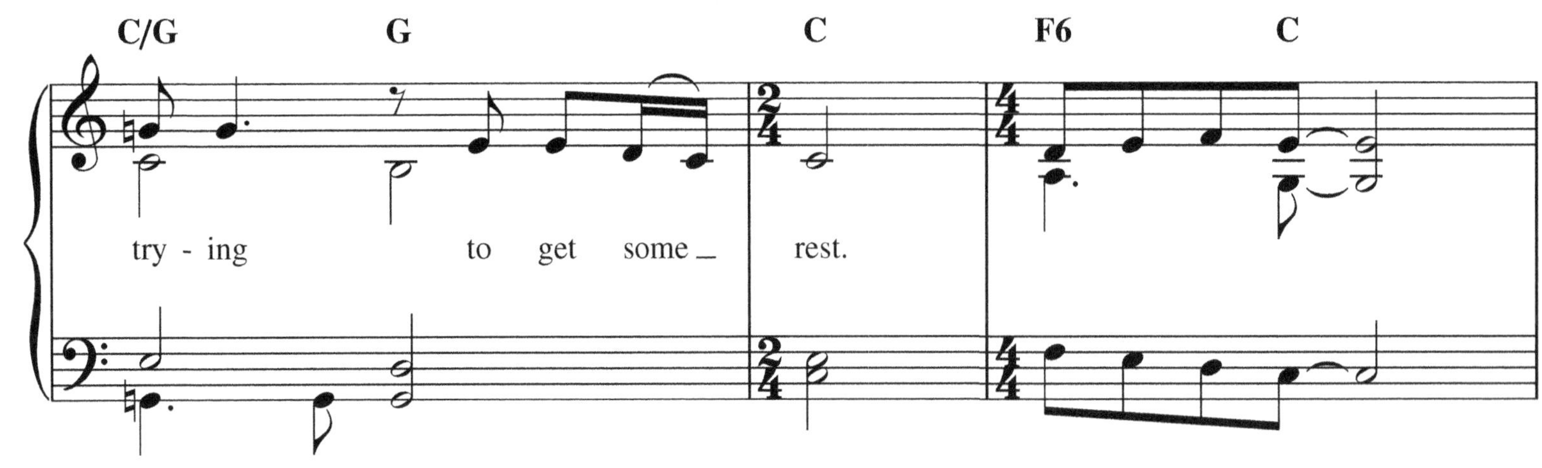

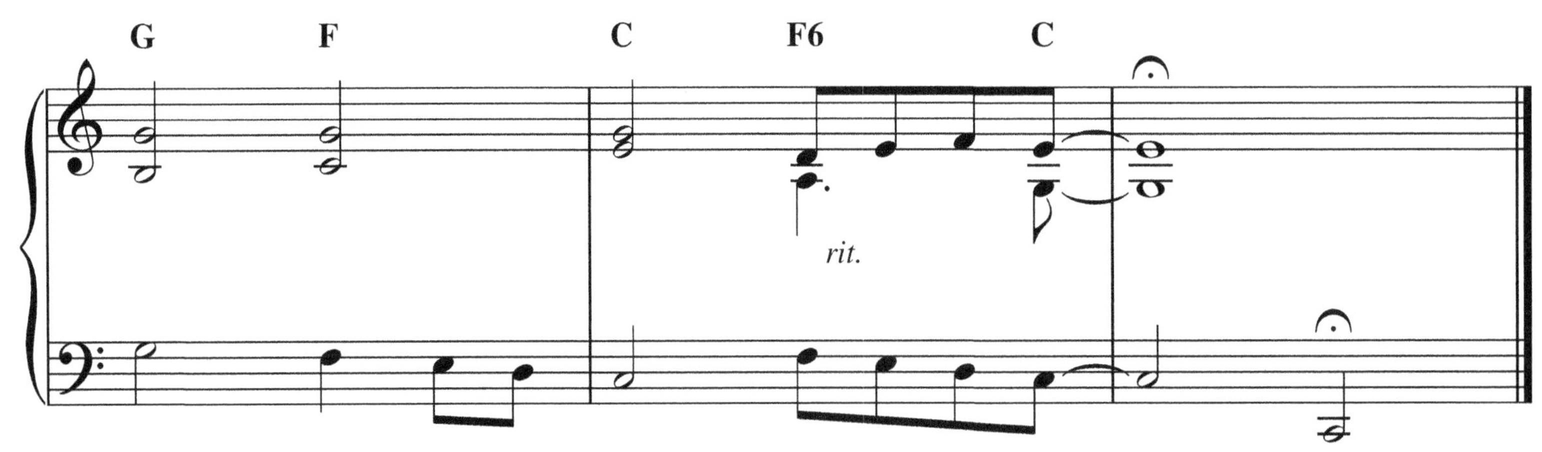

Additional Lyrics

We come on the ship they call the Mayflow'r,
We come on the ship that sailed the moon.
We come in the age's most uncertain hours
And sing an American tune.
Oh, and it's alright, it's alright, it's alright.
You can't be forever blessed.
Still, tomorrow's goin' to be another working day,
And I'm trying to get some rest.
That's all, I'm trying to get some rest.

BRIDGE OVER TROUBLED WATER

Words and Music by
PAUL SIMON

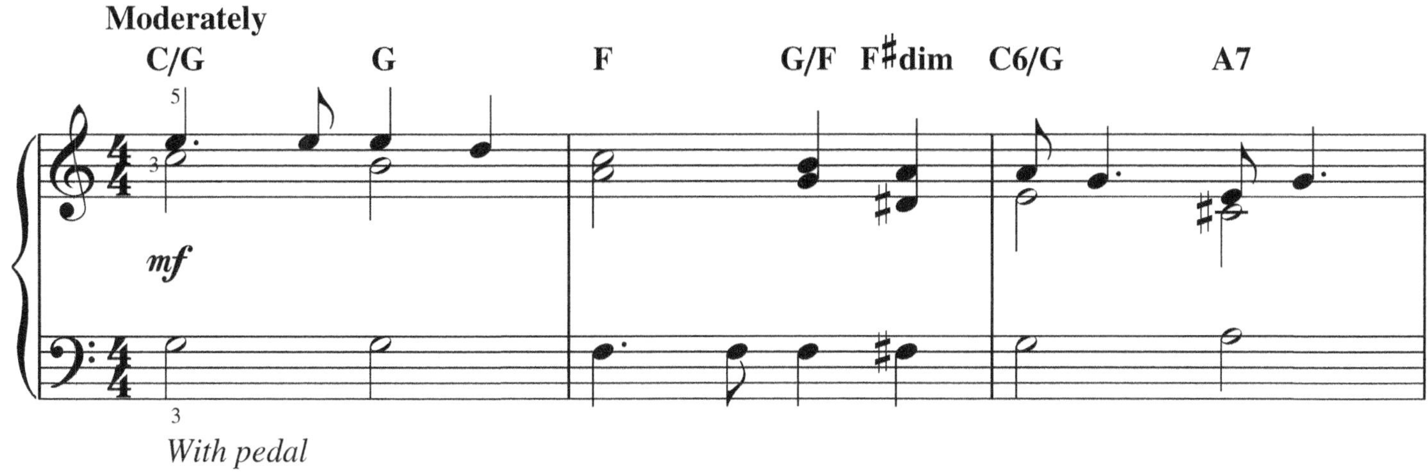

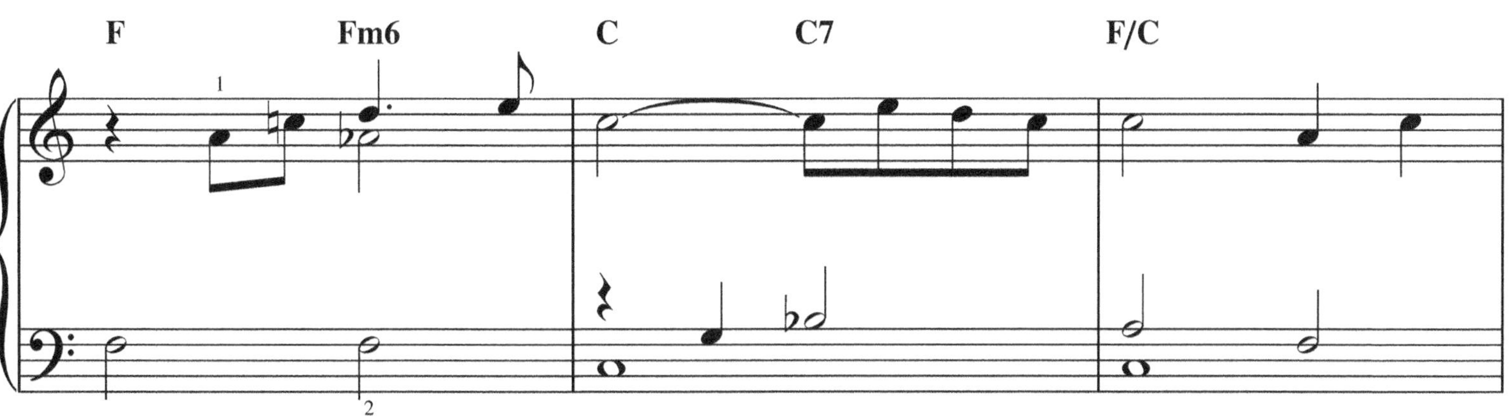

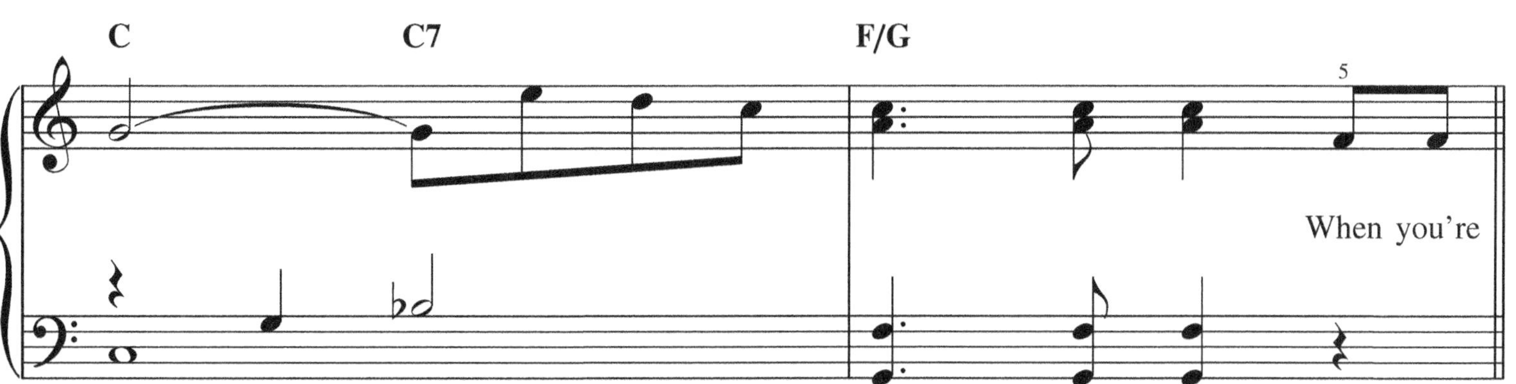

C
F/C
C
wea - ry,
feel - in'
small,
down and out,
when you're on the
street,

F
B♭/D
F
Cmaj7
Dm7
when tears are
in
your
eyes,
I'll
when eve - ning
falls
so
hard,
I

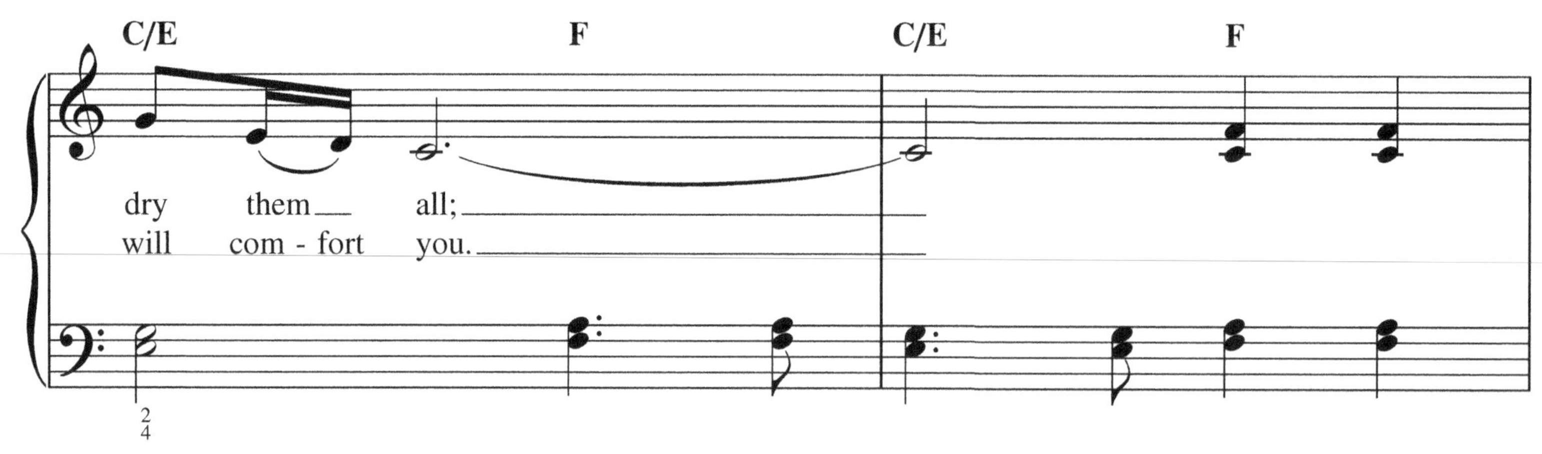
C/E
F
C/E
F
dry them all;
will com - fort you.
2
4

C/E
C
G/B
Am
G
G7
3
I'm on your
side.
Oh, when times get
I'll take your
part.
Oh, when dark - ness
2

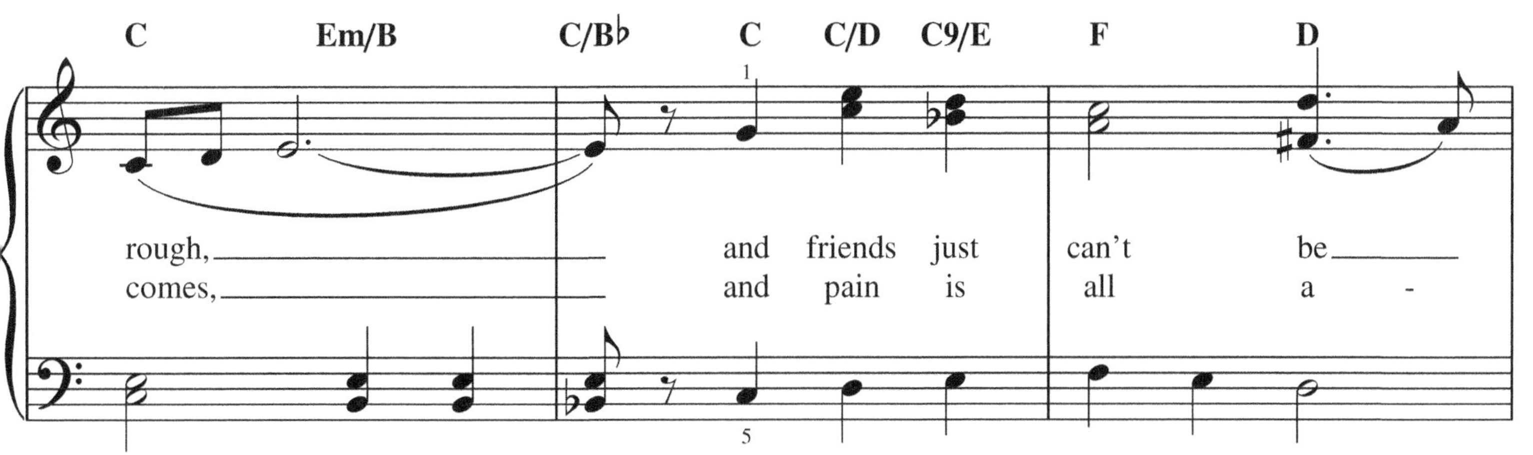
C Em/B C/B♭ C C/D C9/E F D
rough, and friends just can't be
comes, and pain is all a -

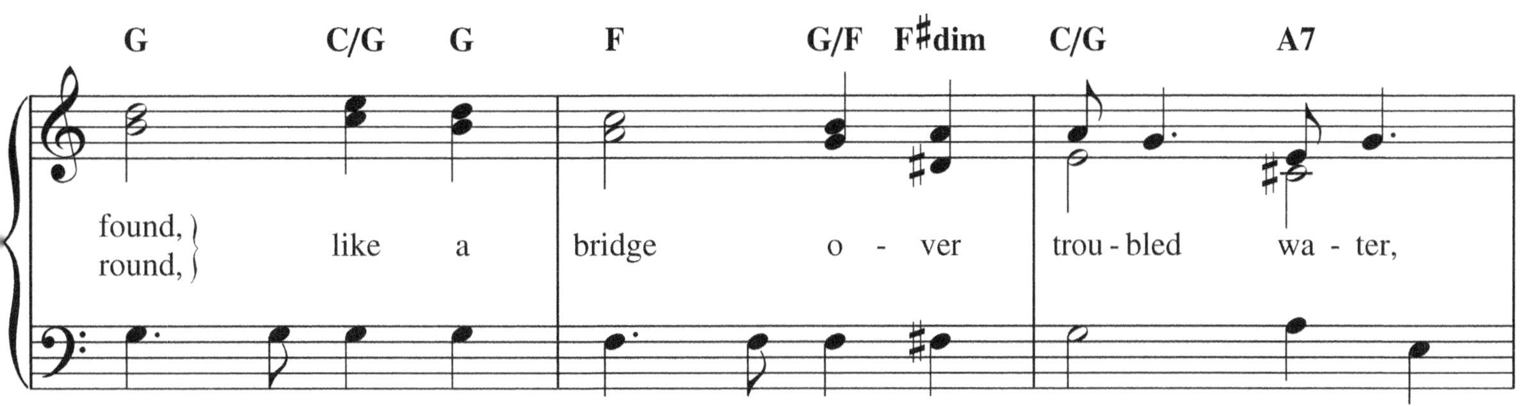
G C/G G F G/F F♯dim C/G A7
found, like a bridge o - ver trou - bled wa - ter,
round,

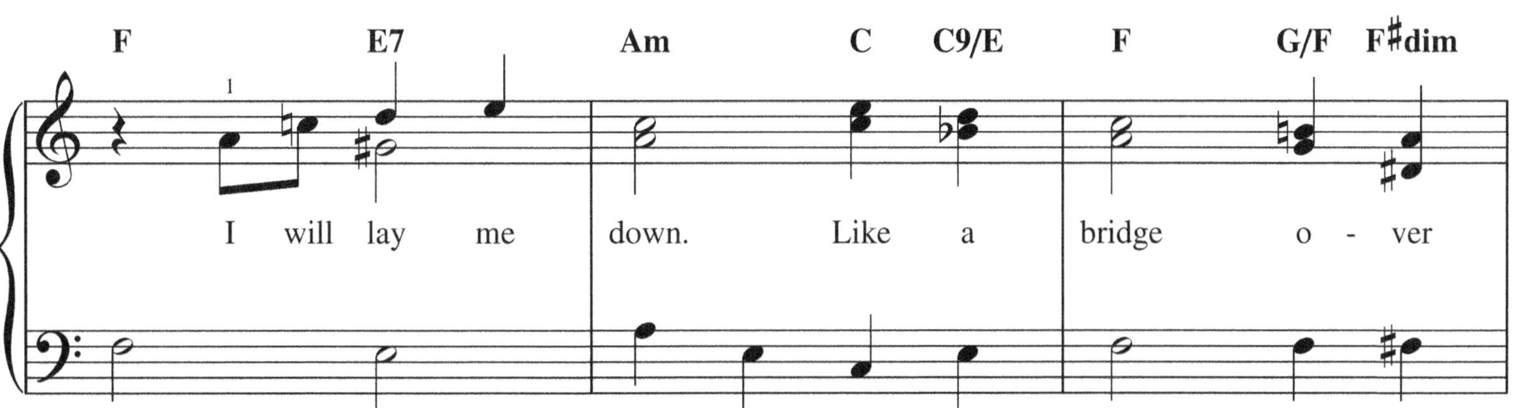
F E7 Am C C9/E F G/F F♯dim
I will lay me down. Like a bridge o - ver

1.
C/G A7 F G9 C
trou - bled wa - ter, I will lay me down.

F/C
B♭/C
F/C
C
F
B♭/C
F/C

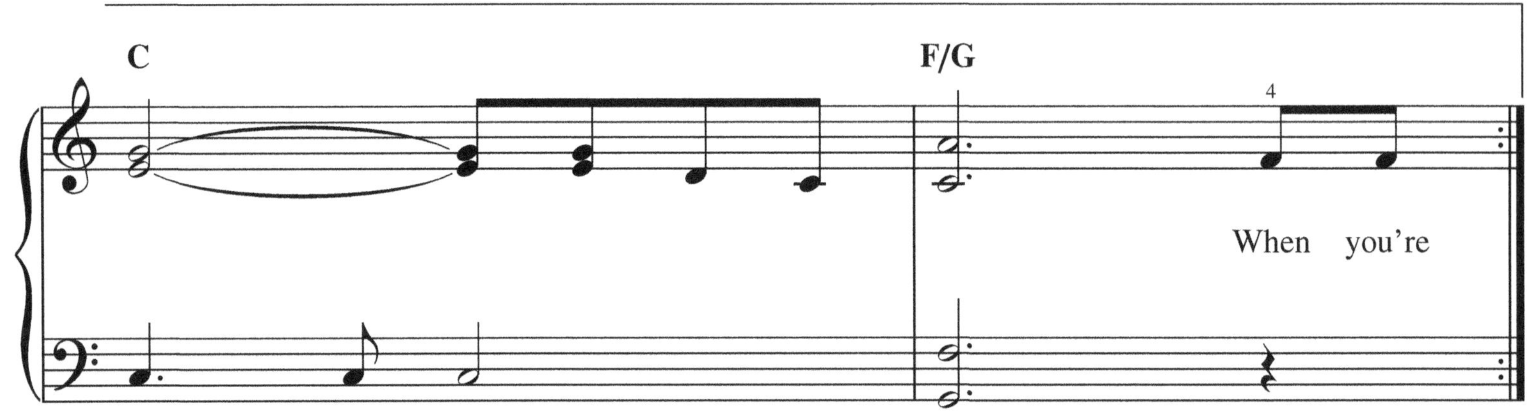
C
F/G
4
When you're

2.
C/G
Am/G
F
E+
E
Am
trou-bled wa - ter,
I will lay me
down.

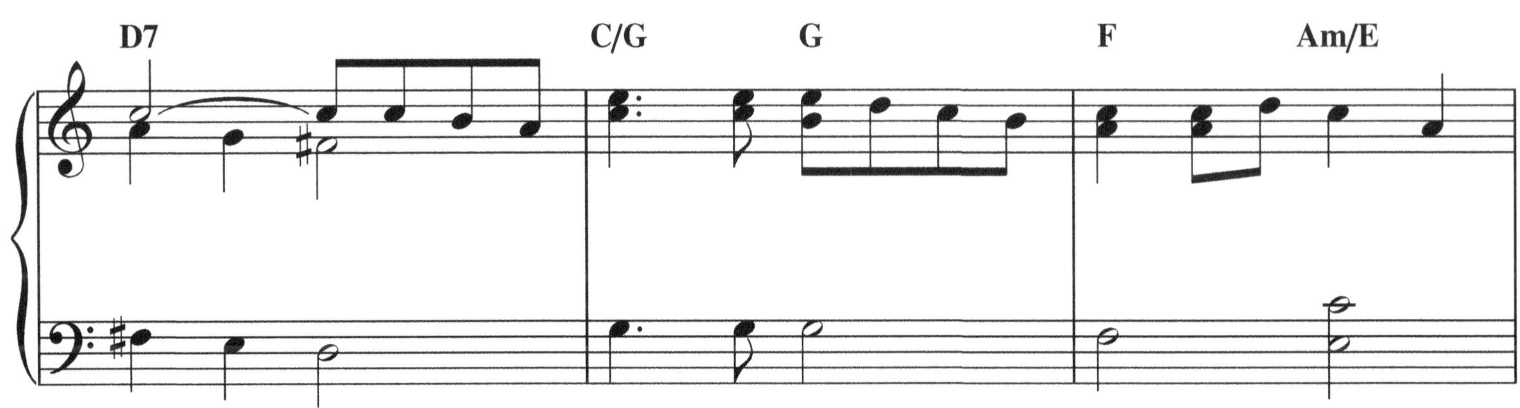
D7
C/G
G
F
Am/E

F
Fm
C
F/C
B♭/C
F/C

C
F
B♭/C
F/C
C

F/G
C
F/C
Sail on, sil - ver girl,
sail on

C
F
B♭/D
F
Cmaj7
by.
Your time has come to

Dm7
C/E
F
C/E
F
shine. All your dreams are on their way.

C/E
C
G/B
Am
G
G7
See how they shine. Oh, if you

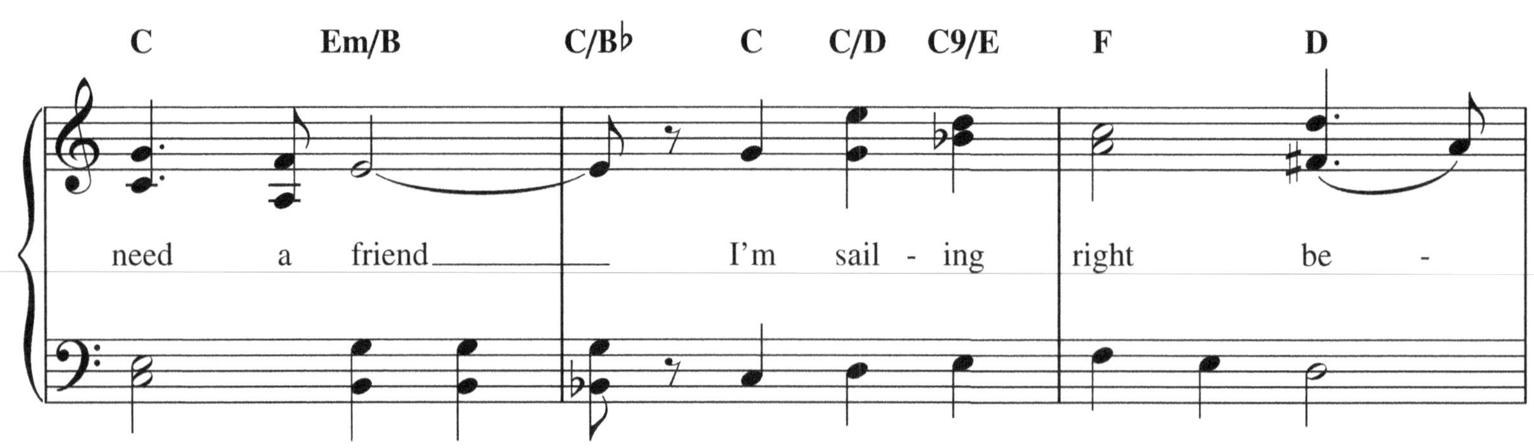
C
Em/B
C/B♭
C
C/D
C9/E
F
D
need a friend I'm sail - ing right be -

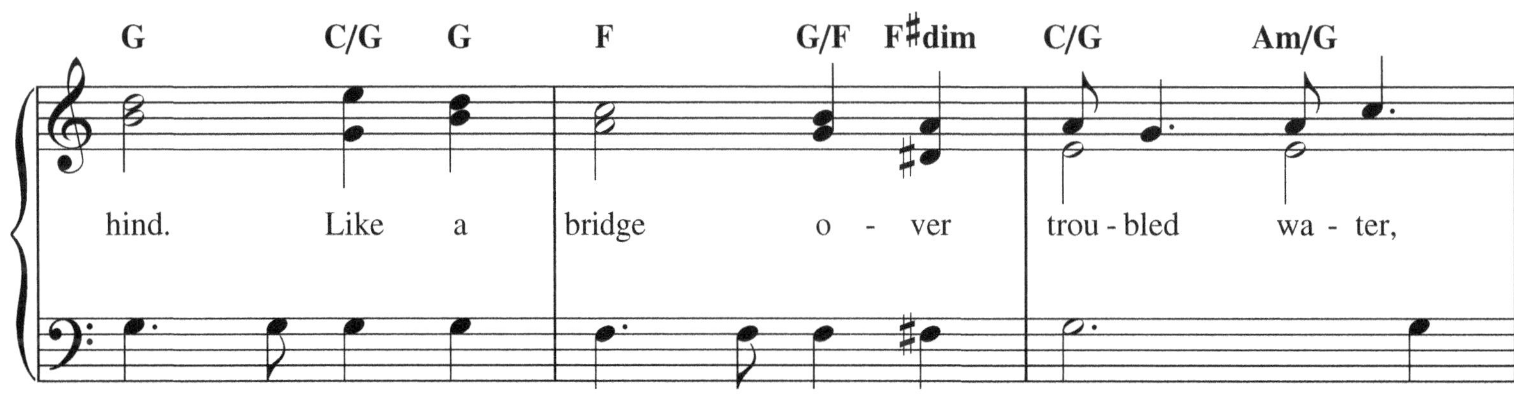
G
C/G
G
F
G/F
F♯dim
C/G
Am/G
hind. Like a bridge o - ver trou - bled wa - ter,

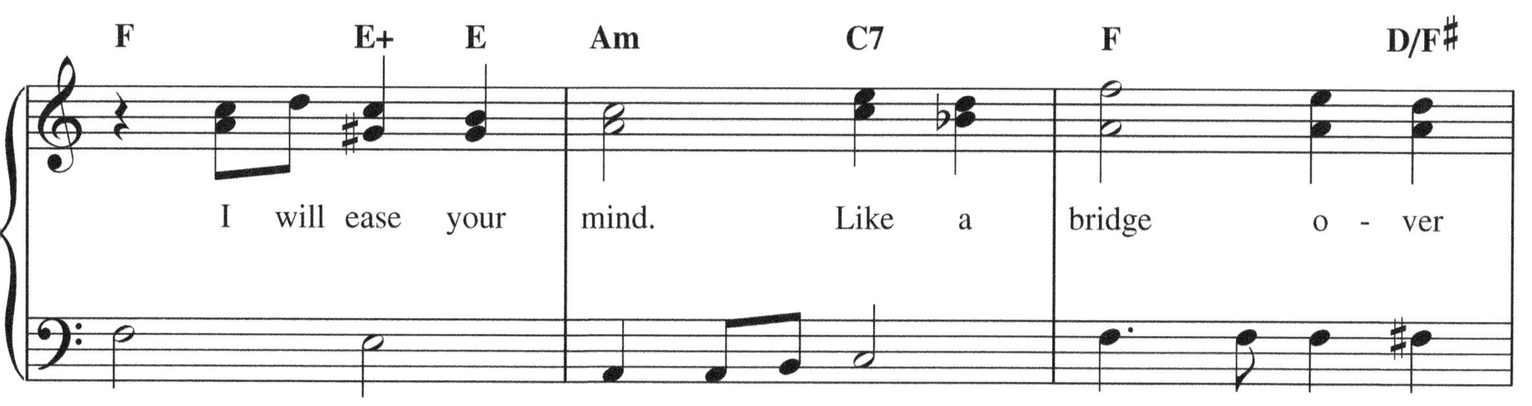
F
E+
E
Am
C7
F
D/F♯
I will ease your mind. Like a bridge o - ver

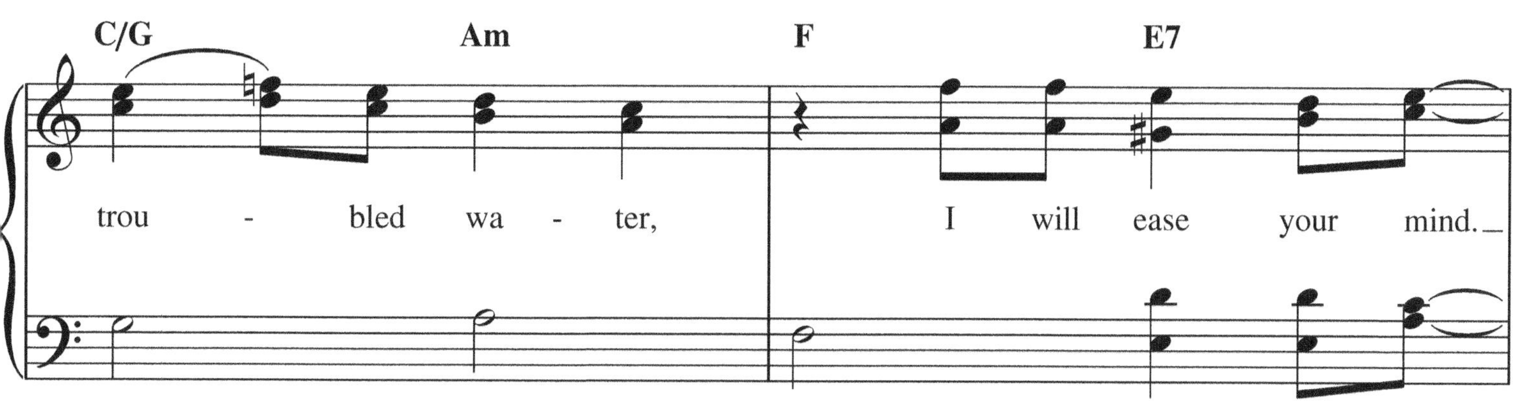
C/G
Am
F
E7
trou - bled wa - ter, I will ease your mind.

Am
F♯m7♭5
C/G
G

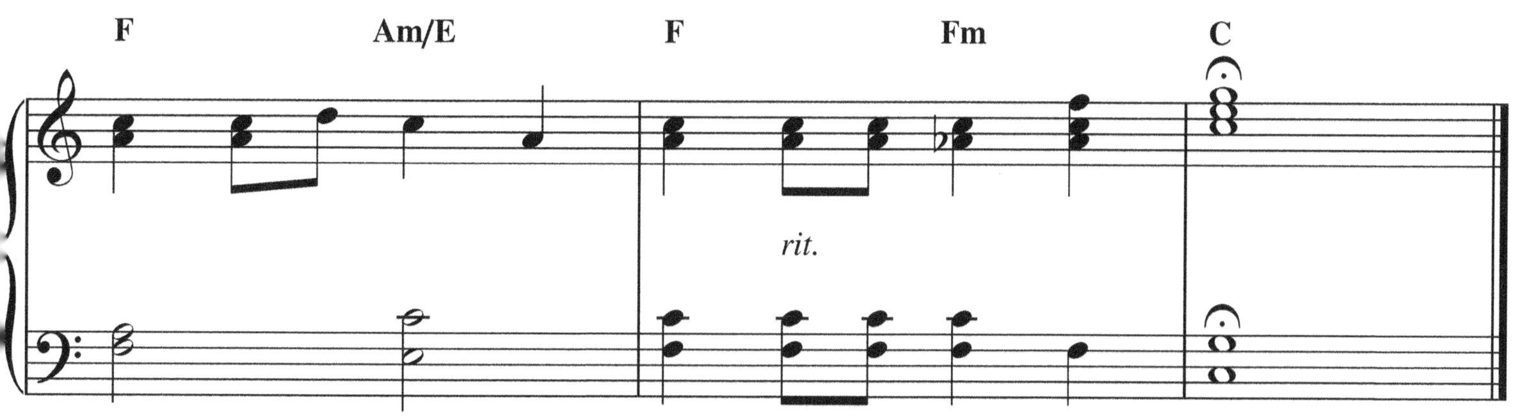
F
Am/E
F
Fm
C
rit.

THE BOXER

Words and Music by
PAUL SIMON

G
F
man hears what he wants to hear, and dis - re - gards the

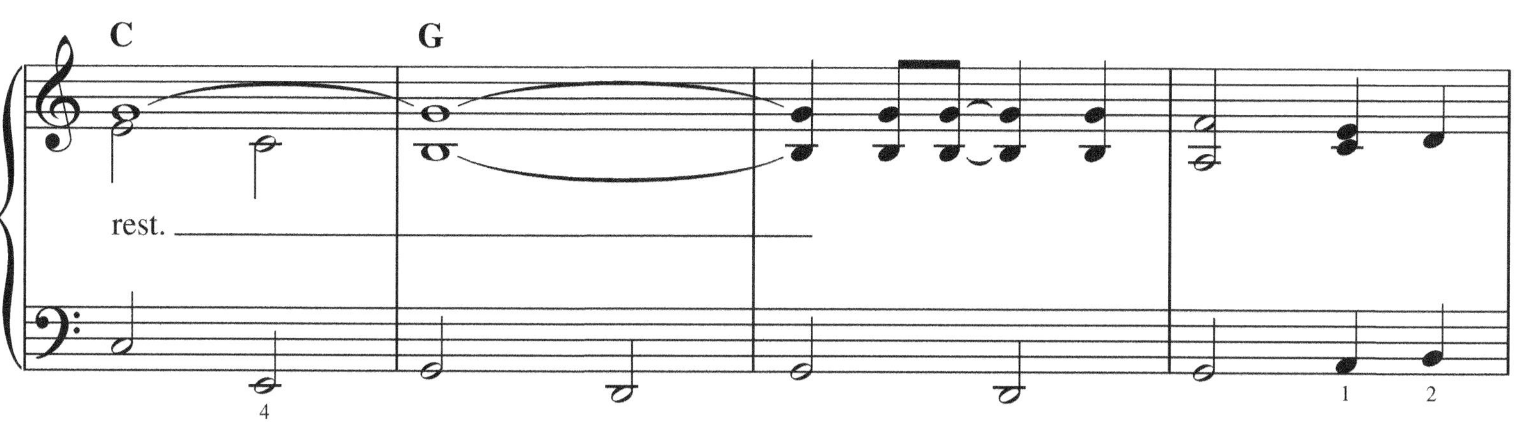
C
G
rest.

C
When I left my home and my fam - i - ly, I was

Am
G
no more than a boy in the com - pa - ny of stran - gers in the

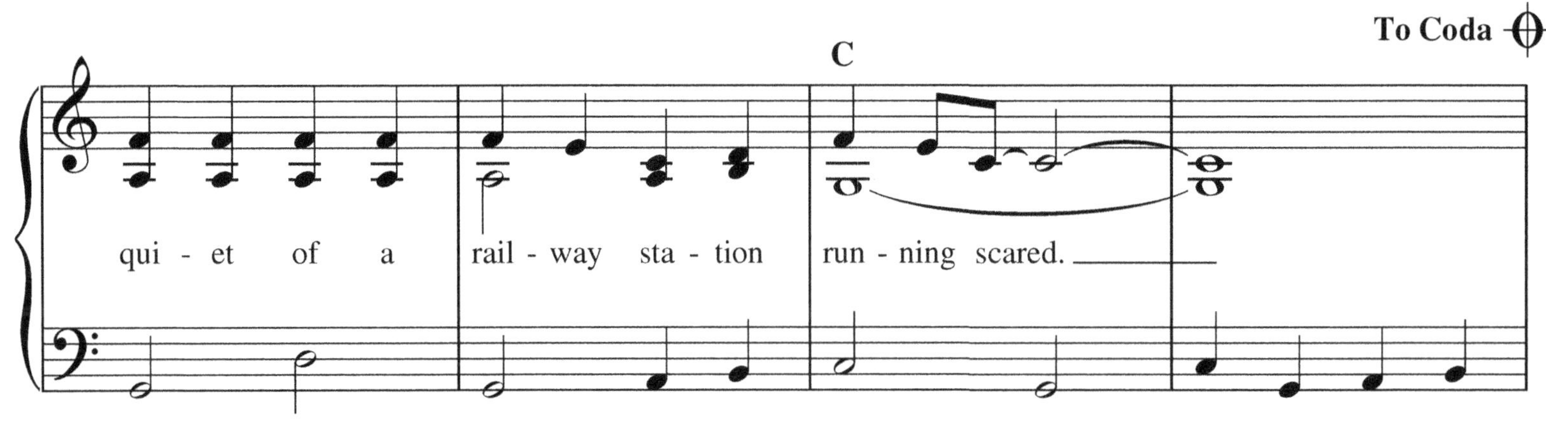
To Coda
C
qui - et of a rail - way sta - tion run - ning scared.

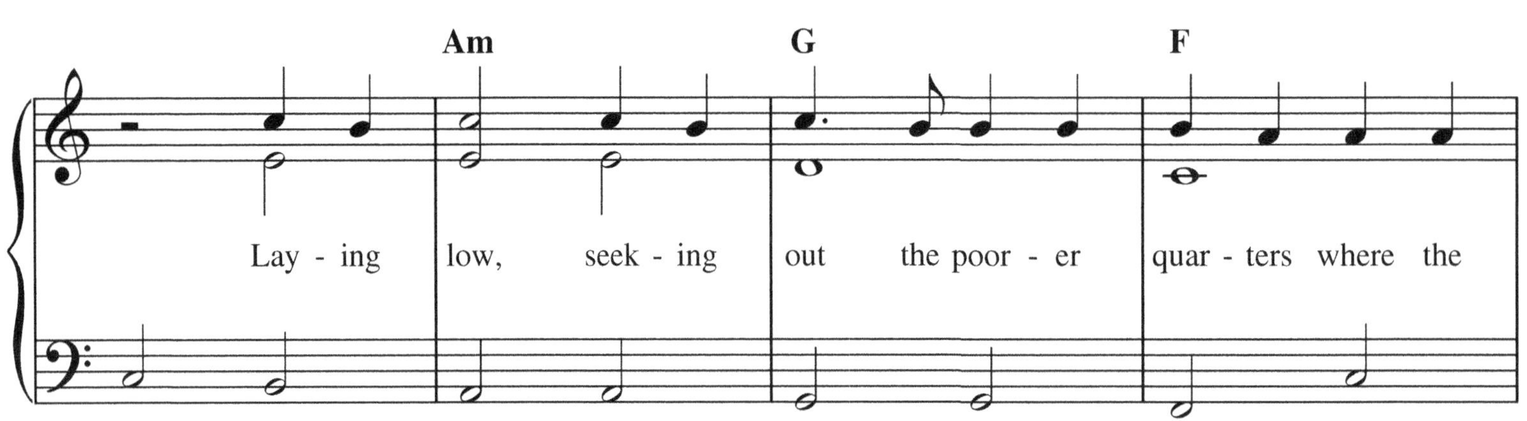
Am
G
F
Lay - ing low, seek - ing out the poor - er quar - ters where the

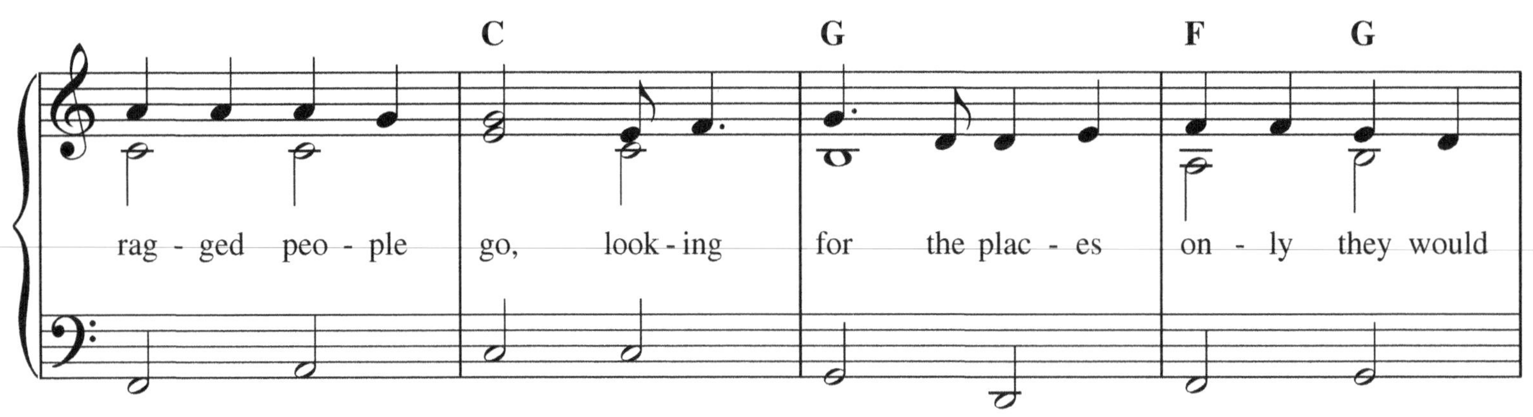
C
G
F
G
rag - ged peo - ple go, look - ing for the plac - es on - ly they would

C
Am
know. Lie - la - lie, lie - la -

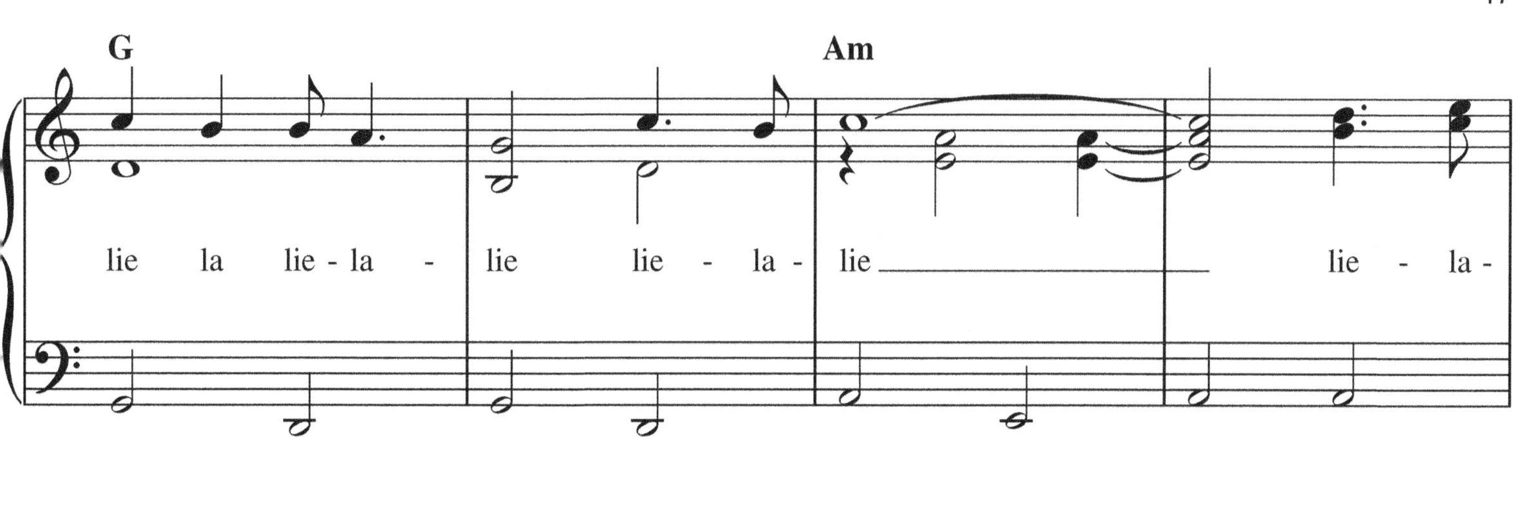
G
Am
lie la lie - la - lie lie - la - lie lie - la -

G
C
lie la la la la lie la la la la lie.

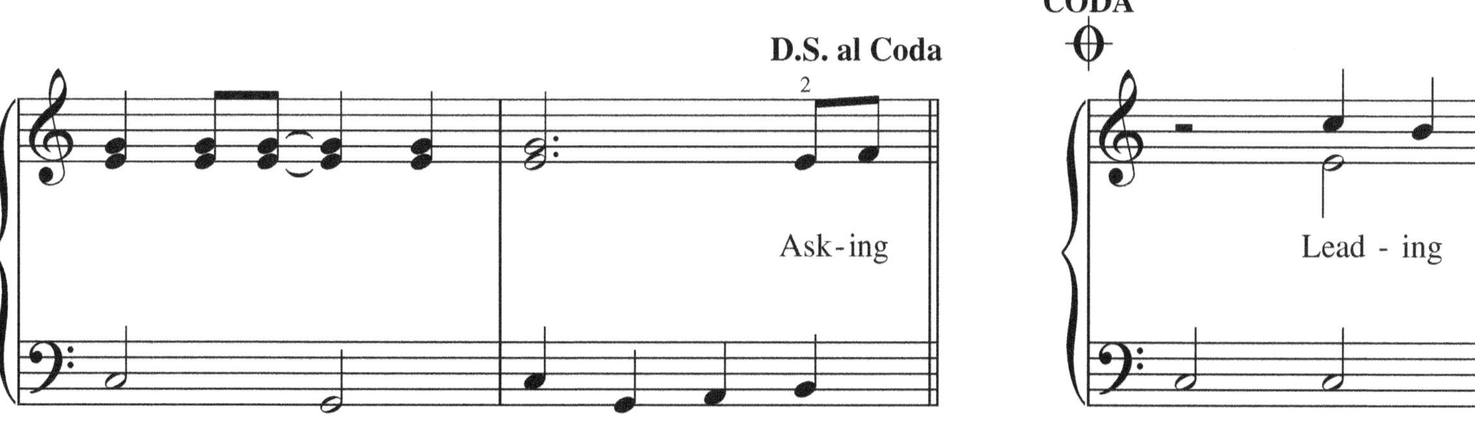
D.S. al Coda
CODA
Ask-ing
Lead - ing

Em
Am
G
me, go - ing home.

C
In the clear - ing stands a box - er, and a fight - er by his

Am
G
trade, and he car - ries the re - mind - ers of ev - 'ry glove that

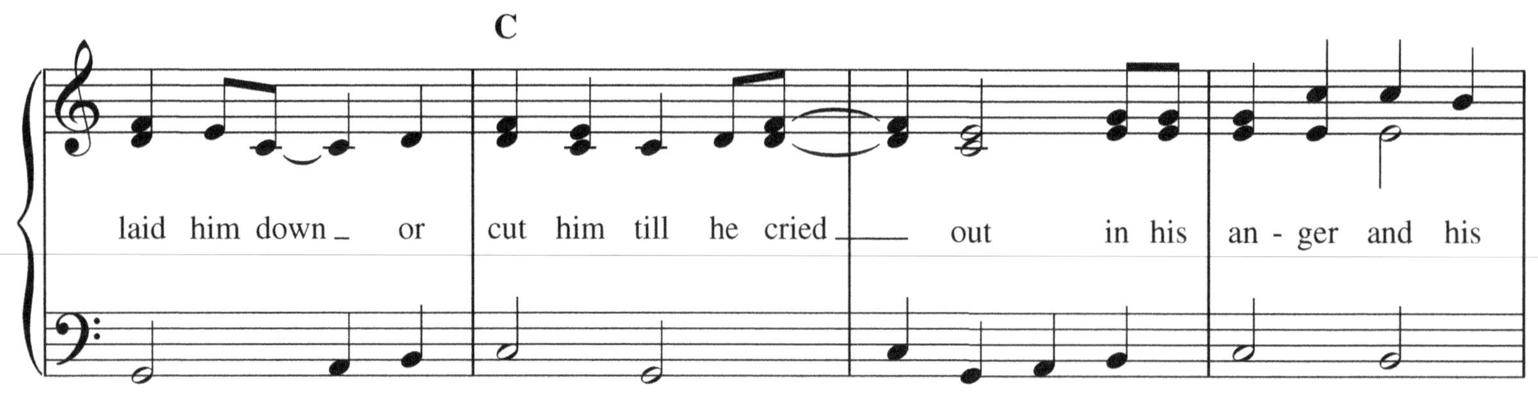
C
laid him down or cut him till he cried out in his an - ger and his

Am
G
F
shame, "I am leav - ing, I am leav - ing." But the fight - er still re - mains.

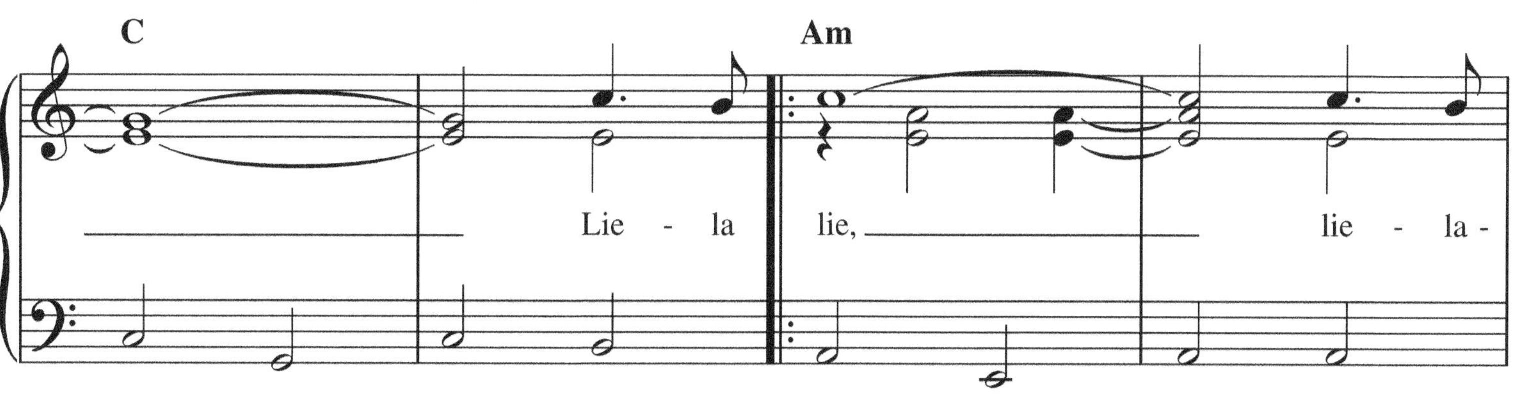

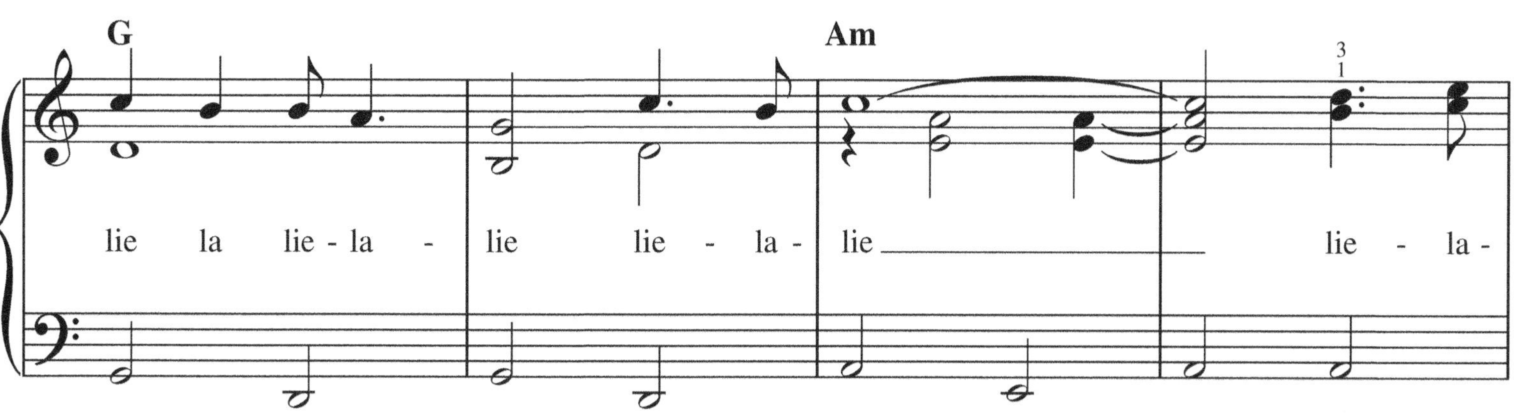

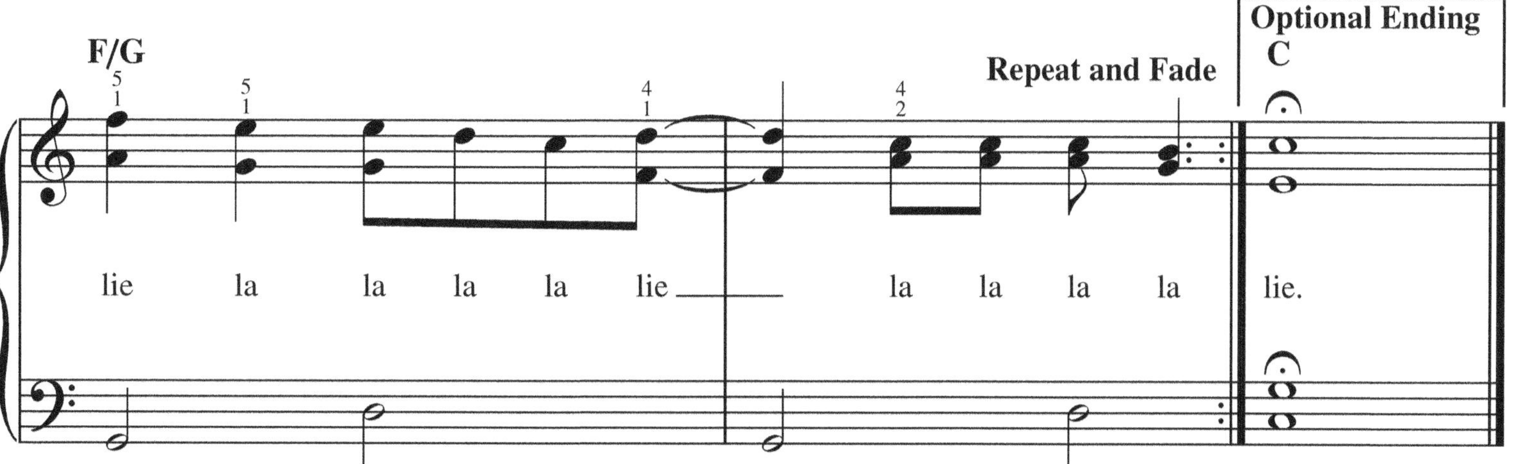

Additional Lyrics

Asking only workman's wages
I come looking for a job,
But I get no offers,
Just a come-on from the whores on
Seventh Avenue.
I do declare, there were times when I was so
Lonesome I took some comfort there.
Ooo-la-la la-la la la.
Then I'm laying out my winter clothes
And wishing I was gone, going home
Where the New York City winters aren't bleeding me.

CECILIA

Words and Music by
PAUL SIMON

G
C
Mak-ing love in the af - ter - noon with Ce -

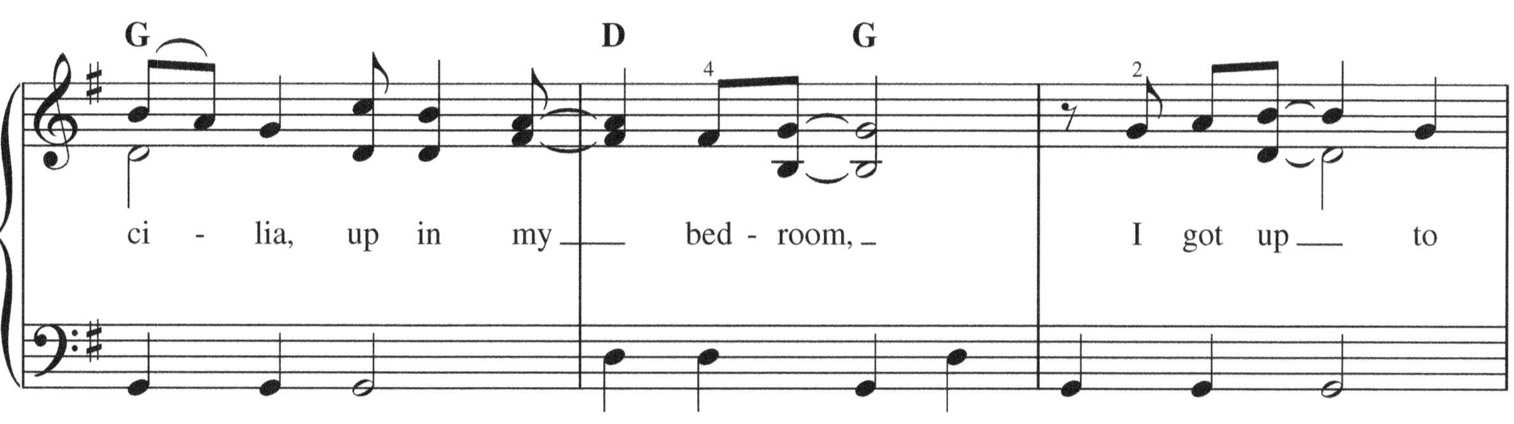
G
D
G
4
2
ci - lia, up in my bed - room, I got up to

C
G
wash my face when I come back to bed, some-one's tak -

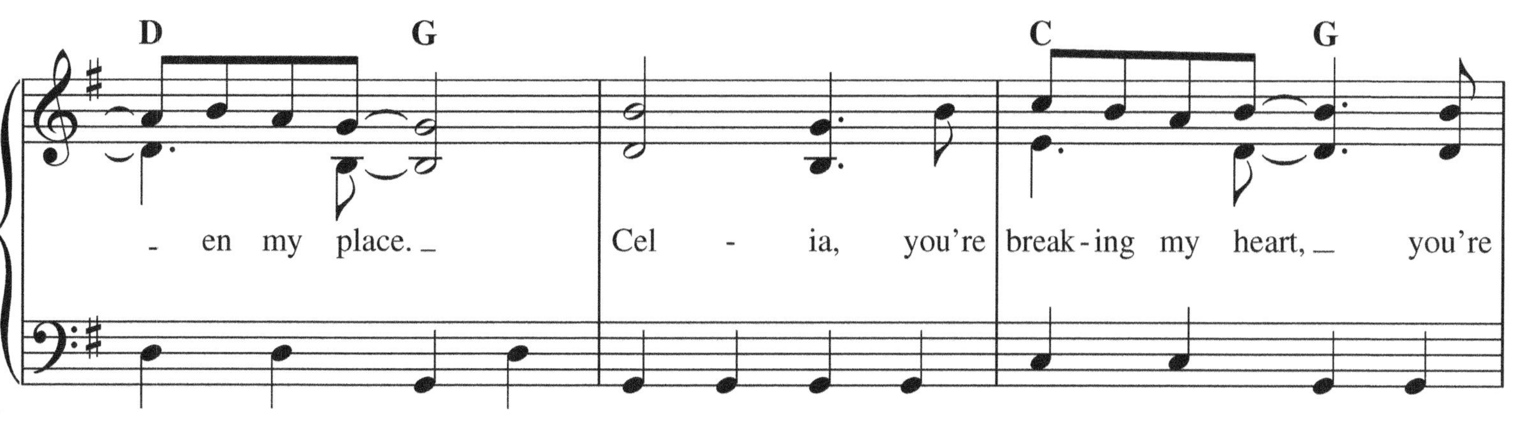
D
G
C
G
- en my place. Cel - ia, you're break-ing my heart, you're

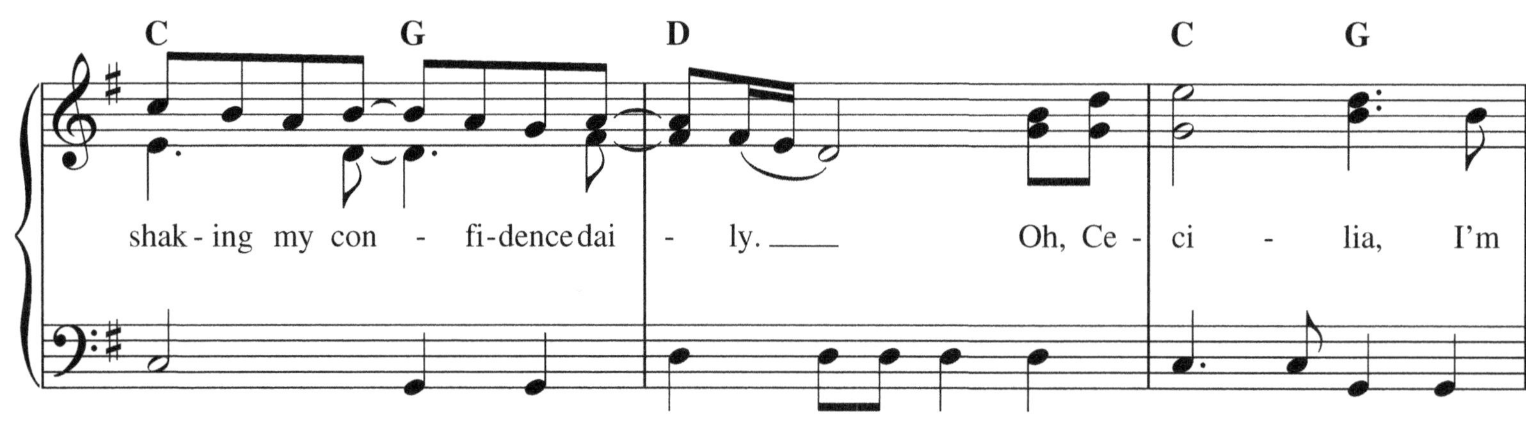
C G D C G
shak - ing my con - fi-dence dai - ly. Oh, Ce - ci - lia, I'm

C G C G
down on my knees, I'm beg - ging you please to come home.

D G C G
Come on home. Poh poh poh poh poh poh poh

C G/B Am7 G D7 C G
poh poh poh poh poh poh. Ju - bi - la - tion, she

C
G
C
G
loves me a - gain, I
fall on the floor and I'm laugh -

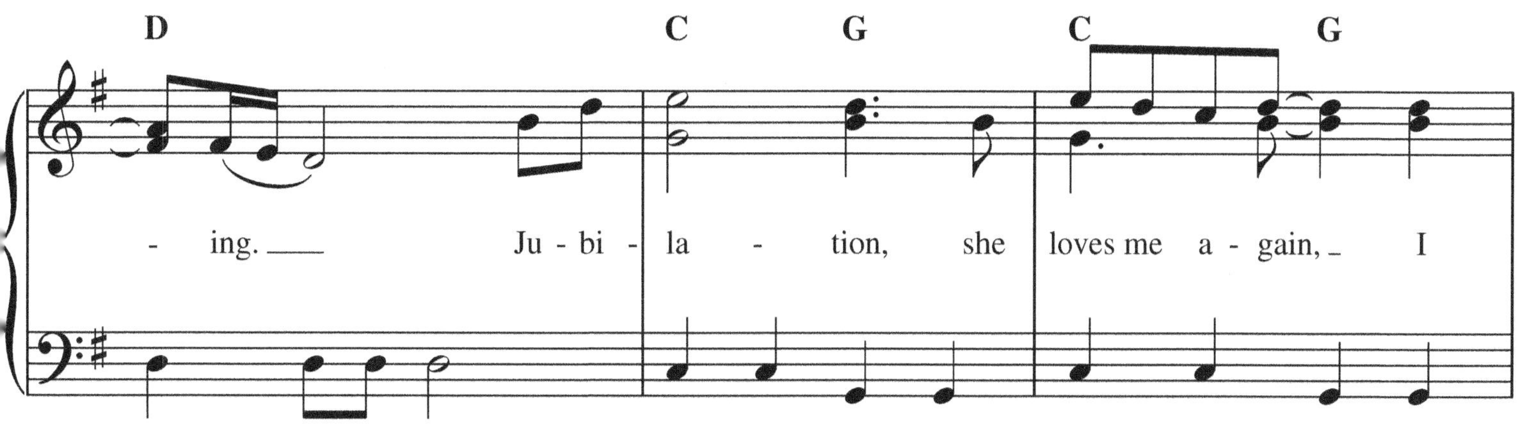
D
C
G
C
G
- ing. Ju - bi -
la - tion, she
loves me a - gain, I

C
G
D
fall on the floor and I'm laugh
- ing. Come on home.

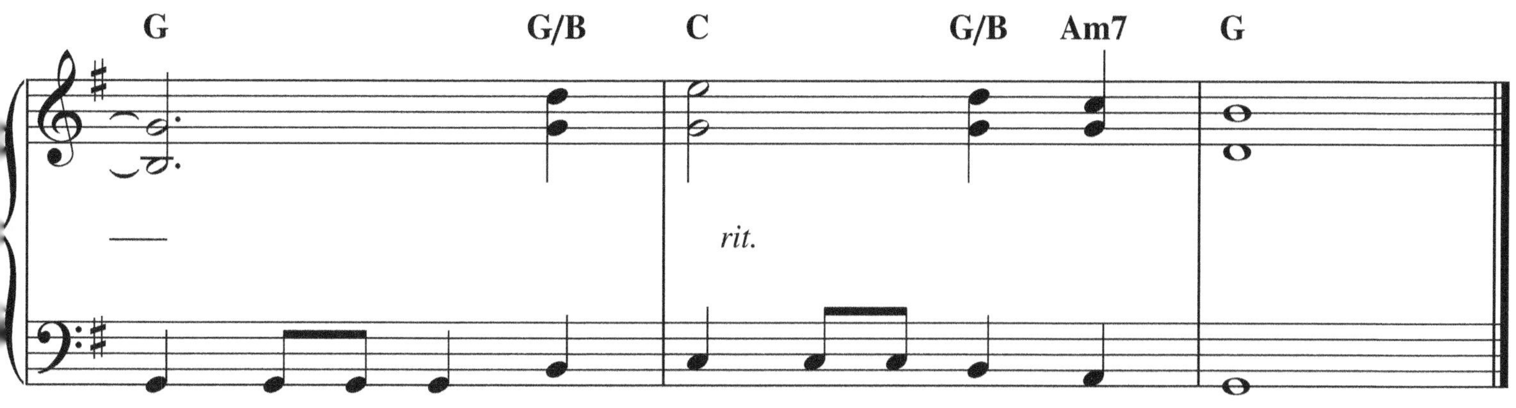
G
G/B
C
G/B
Am7
G
rit.

FIFTY WAYS TO LEAVE YOUR LOVER

Words and Music by
PAUL SIMON

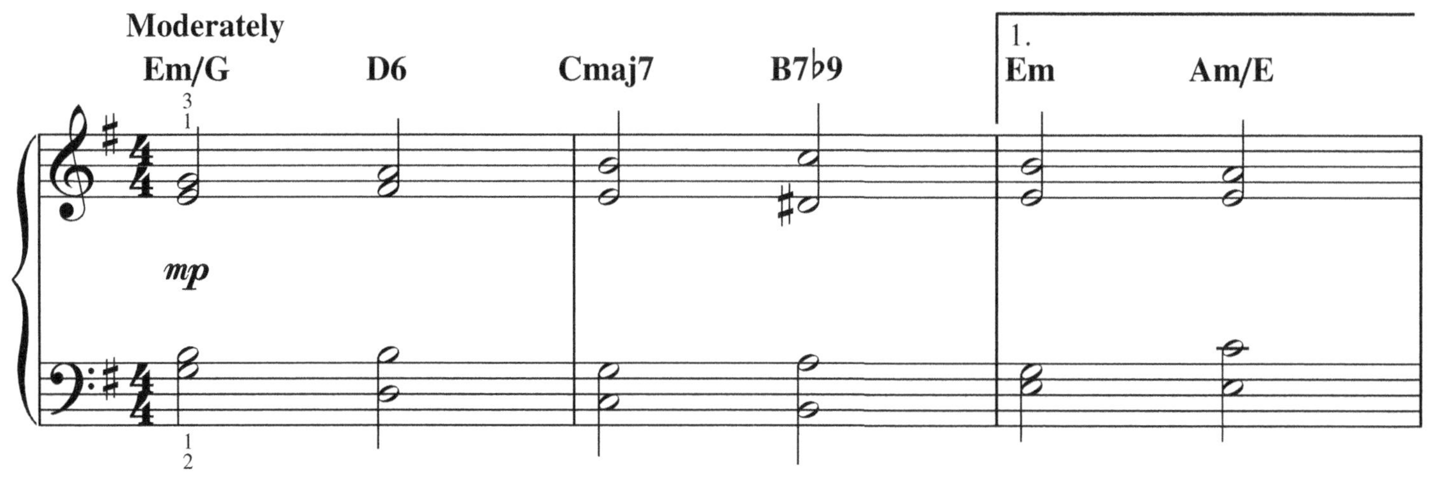

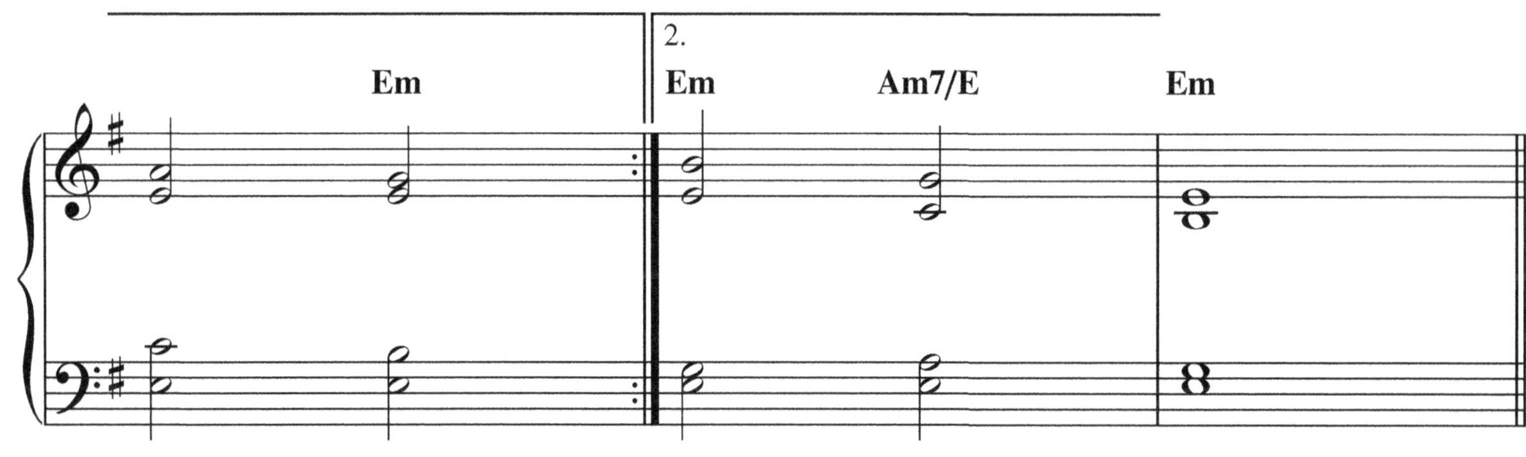

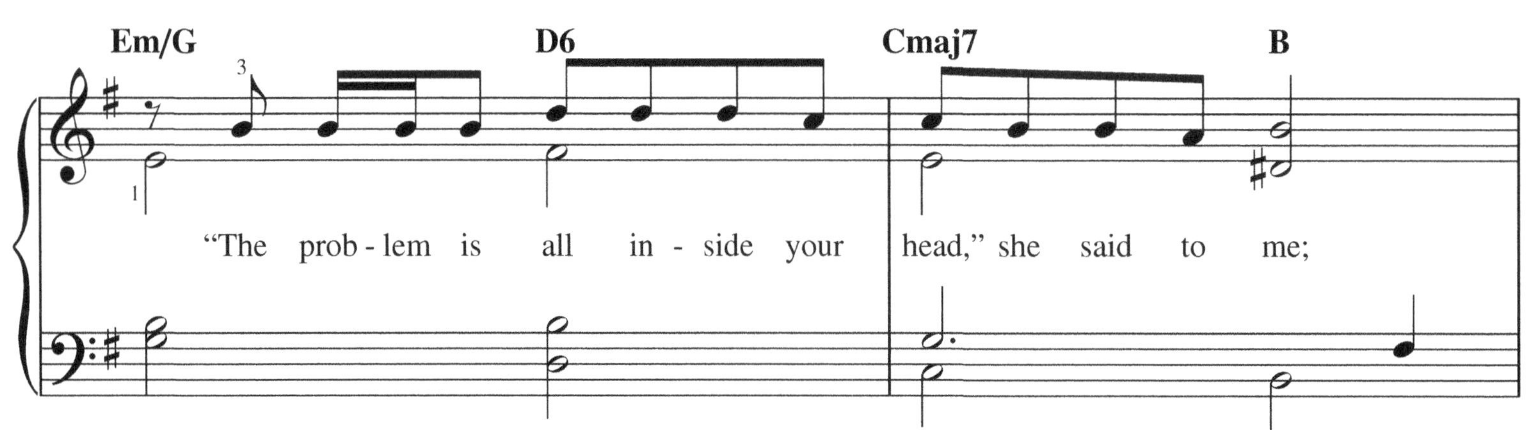

Em
D♯dim
Cm6
B7
"the an - swer is eas - y if you take it log - i - c'lly.
Em
D6
Cmaj7
B7
I'd like to help you in your strug - gle to be free; there must be
Em
Am7
Em
Cmaj7
B
fif - ty ways to leave your lov - er."
Em
D6
Cmaj7
B7
She said, "It's real - ly not my hab - it to in - trude; fur - ther
She said, "Why don't we both just sleep on it to - night; and I

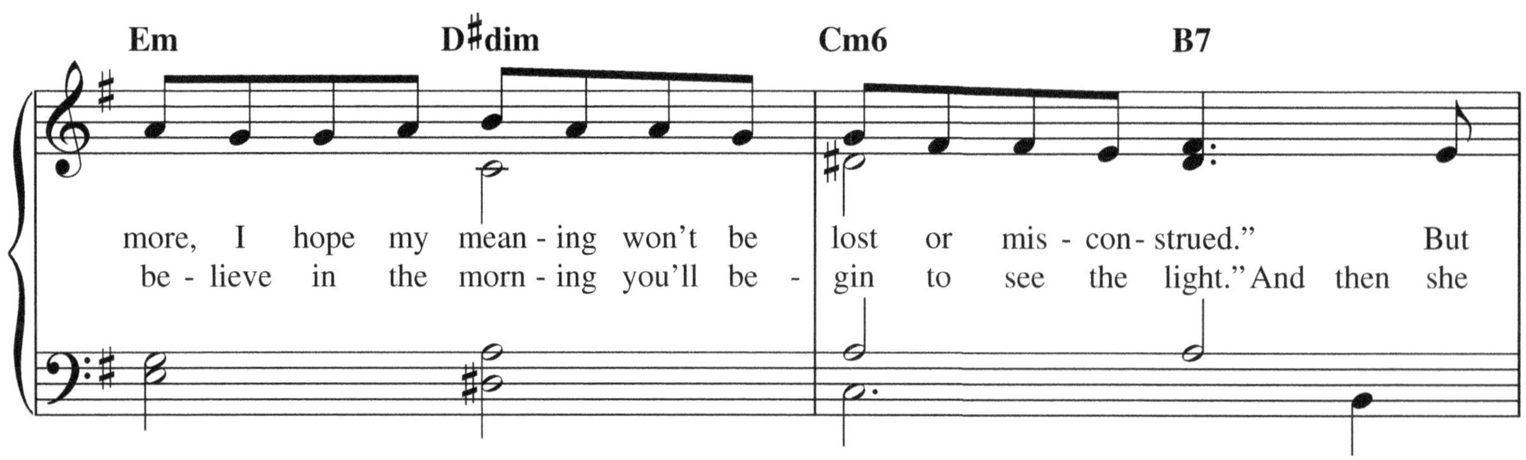
Em
D♯dim
Cm6
B7
more, I hope my mean - ing won't be
lost or mis - con - strued." But
be - lieve in the morn - ing you'll be -
gin to see the light." And then she

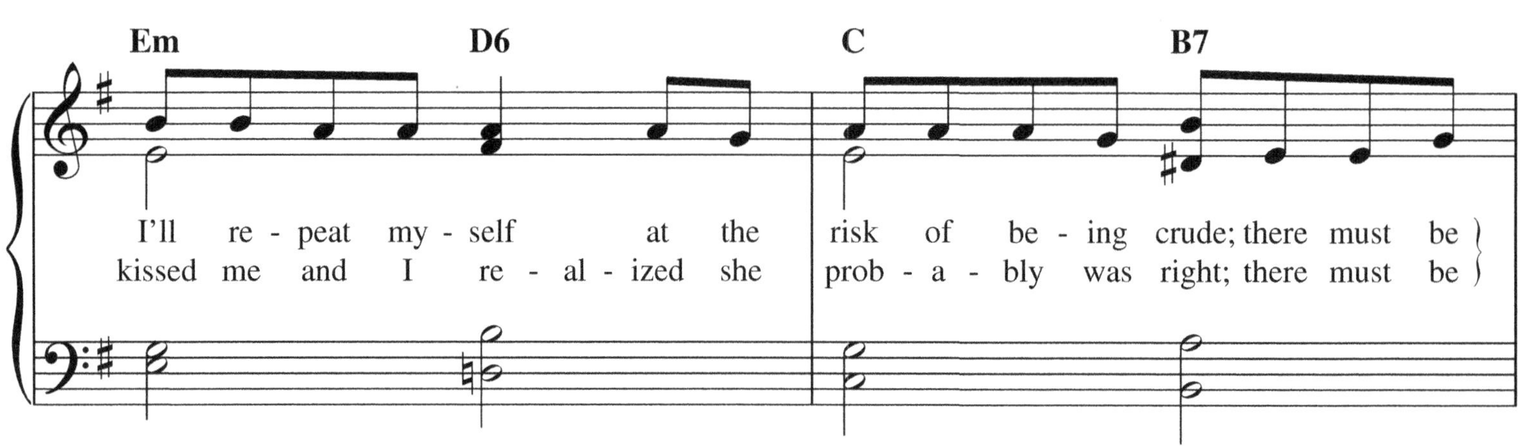
Em
D6
C
B7
I'll re - peat my - self at the
risk of be - ing crude; there must be
kissed me and I re - al - ized she
prob - a - bly was right; there must be

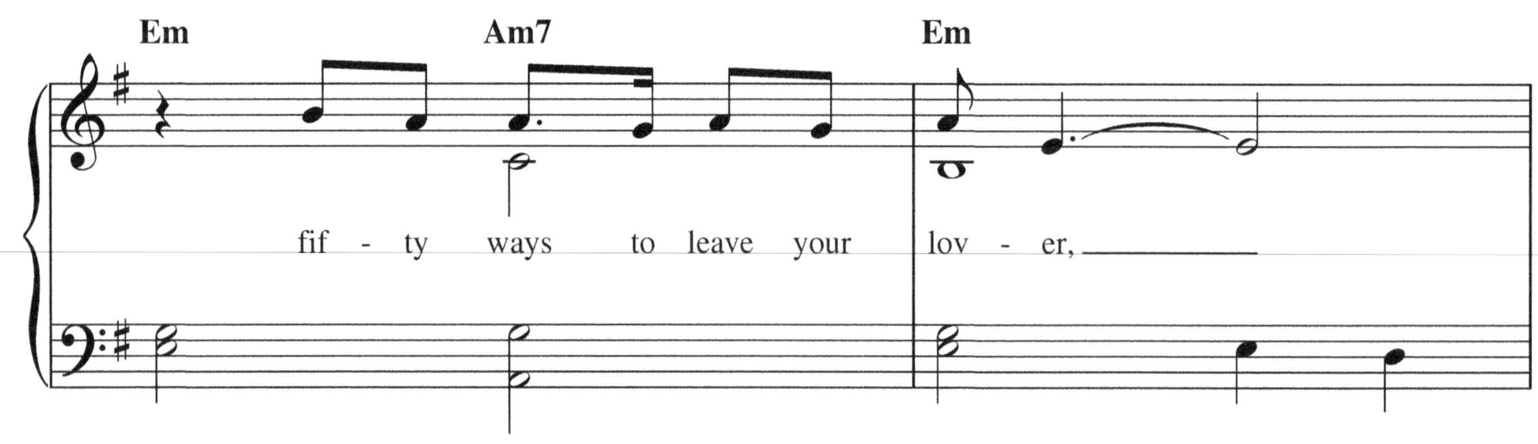
Em
Am7
Em
fif - ty ways to leave your
lov - er,

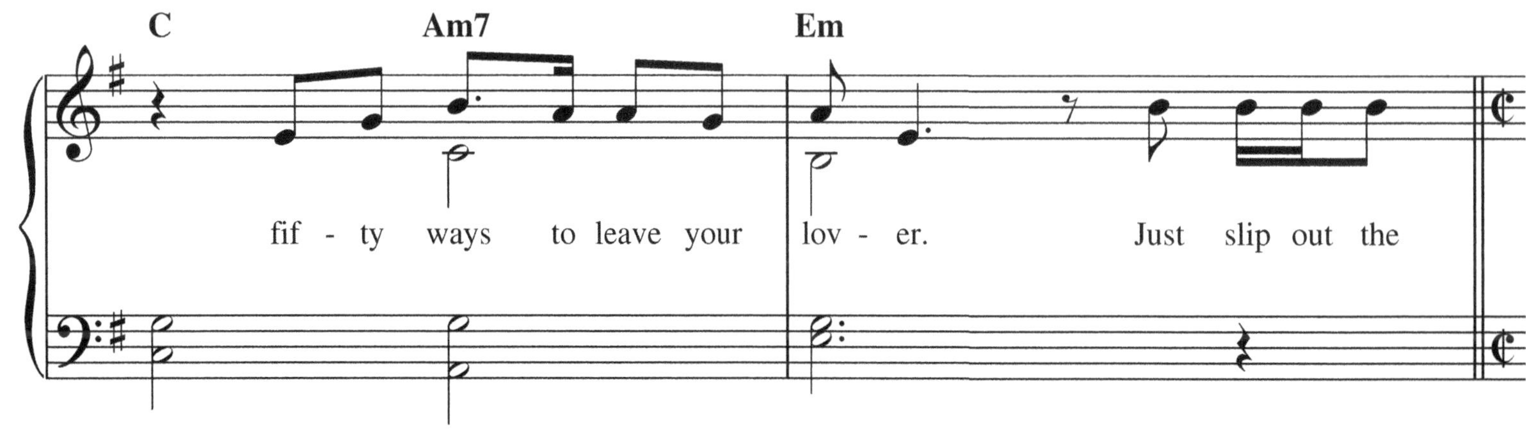
C
Am7
Em
fif - ty ways to leave your
lov - er. Just slip out the

(♩ = 𝅗𝅥 double time)
G
Bb6
back, Jack; make a new plan, Stan;
C7
you don't need to be coy, Roy,
just get your-self free.
just lis - ten to me.
G
5
1
Hop on the bus, Gus;
Bb6
you don't need to dis - cuss much; just drop off the

C7
To Coda
1., 3.
G
key, Lee, and get your - self free.
2.
G
Slip out the
free.
Em/G
D6
She said, "It grieves me so to
Cmaj7
B
Em
D♯dim
see you in such pain; I wish there was
some - thin' I could do to

Cm6
B7
Em
D6
make you smile a - gain."
I said, "I ap - pre - ci - ate that, and
Cmaj7
B7
Em
Am7
would you please ex - plain a - bout the
fif - ty ways?"
D.S. al Coda
(take 1st repeat)
CODA
Em
C
B
G
free.

HOMEWARD BOUND

Words and Music by
PAUL SIMON

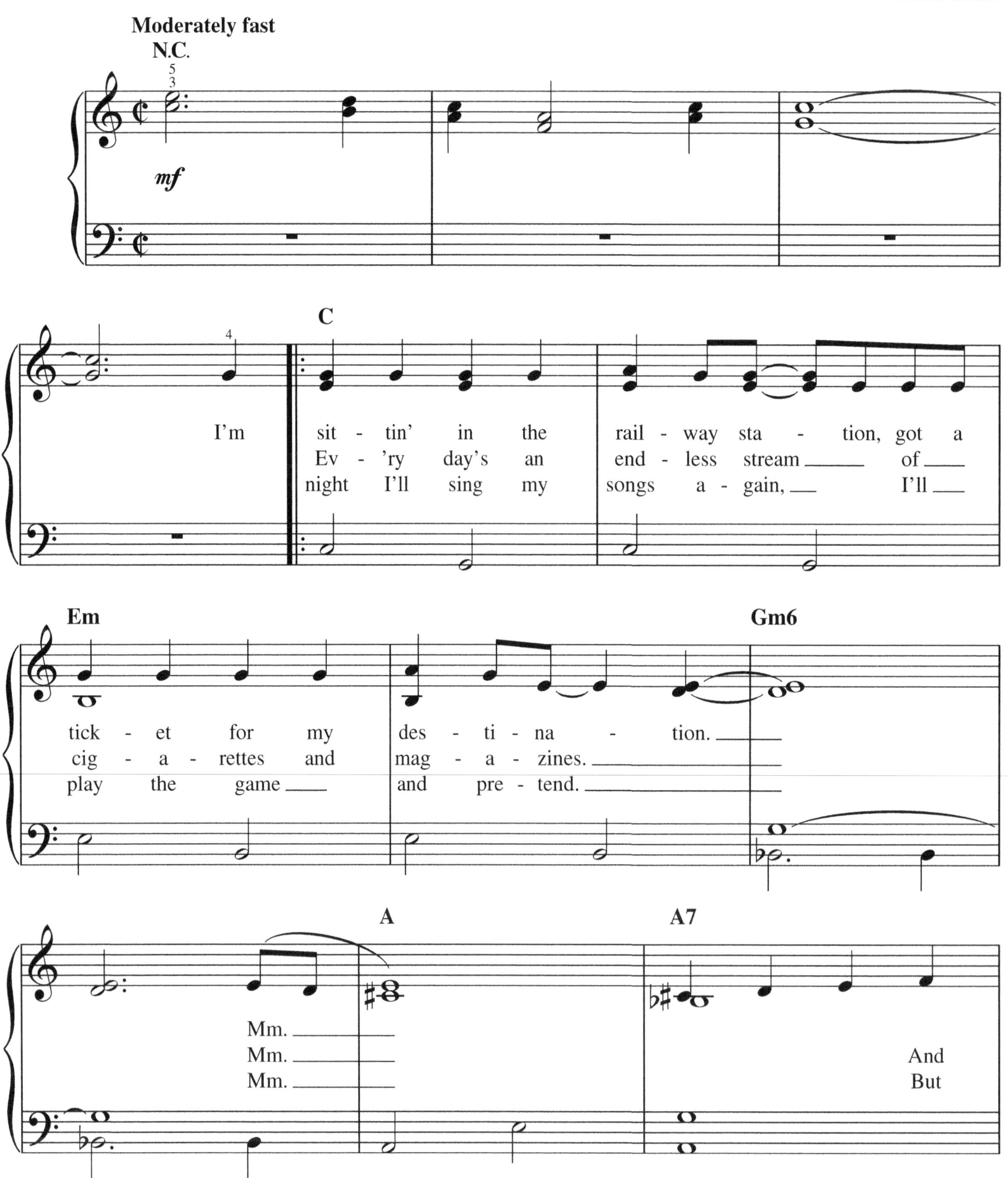

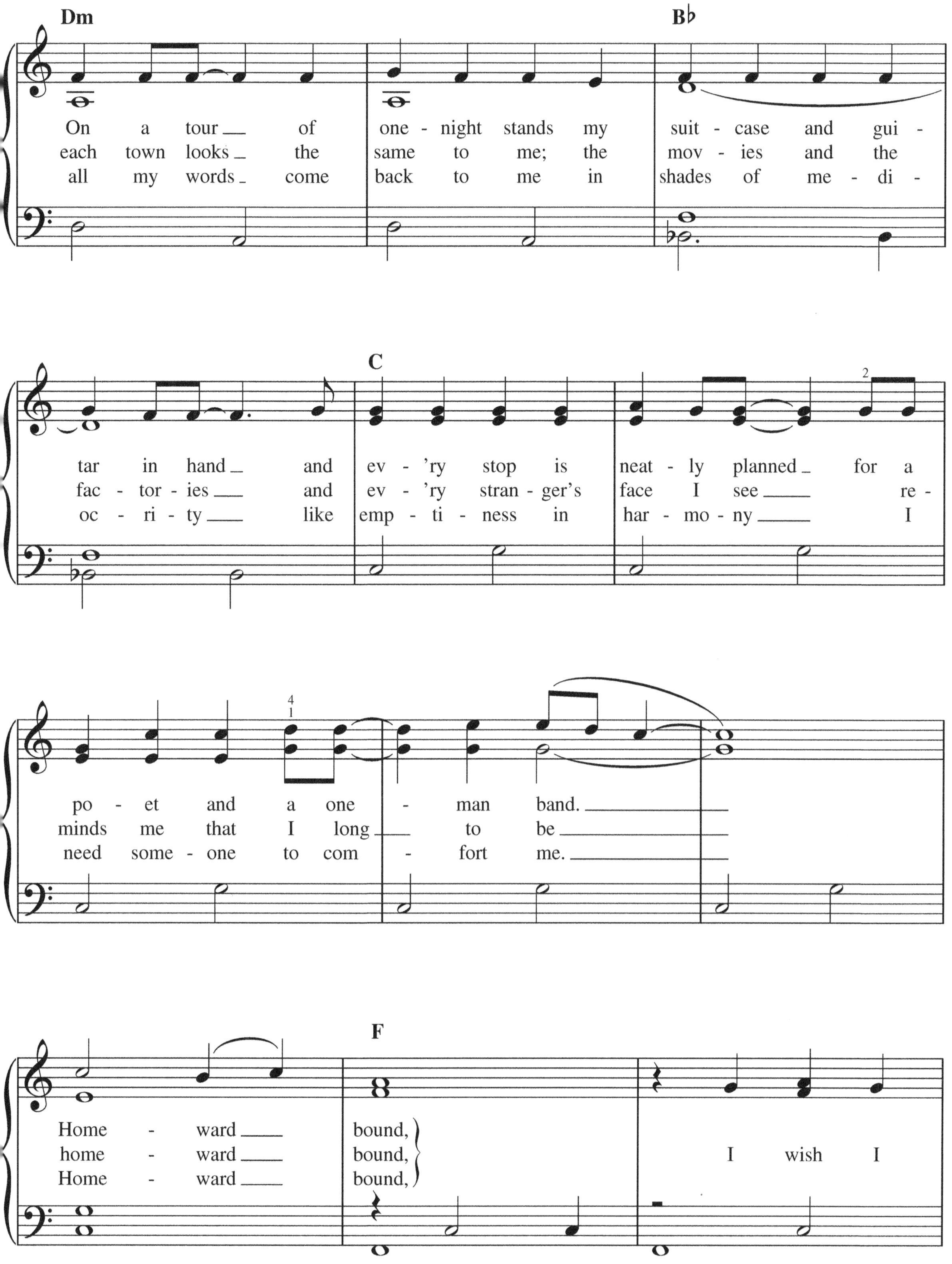

Dm Bb

On a tour __ of one - night stands my suit - case and gui -
each town looks __ the same to me; the mov - ies and the
all my words __ come back to me in shades of me - di -

C

tar in hand __ and ev - 'ry stop is neat - ly planned __ for a
fac - tor - ies __ and ev - 'ry stran - ger's face I see __ re -
oc - ri - ty __ like emp - ti - ness in har - mo - ny __ I

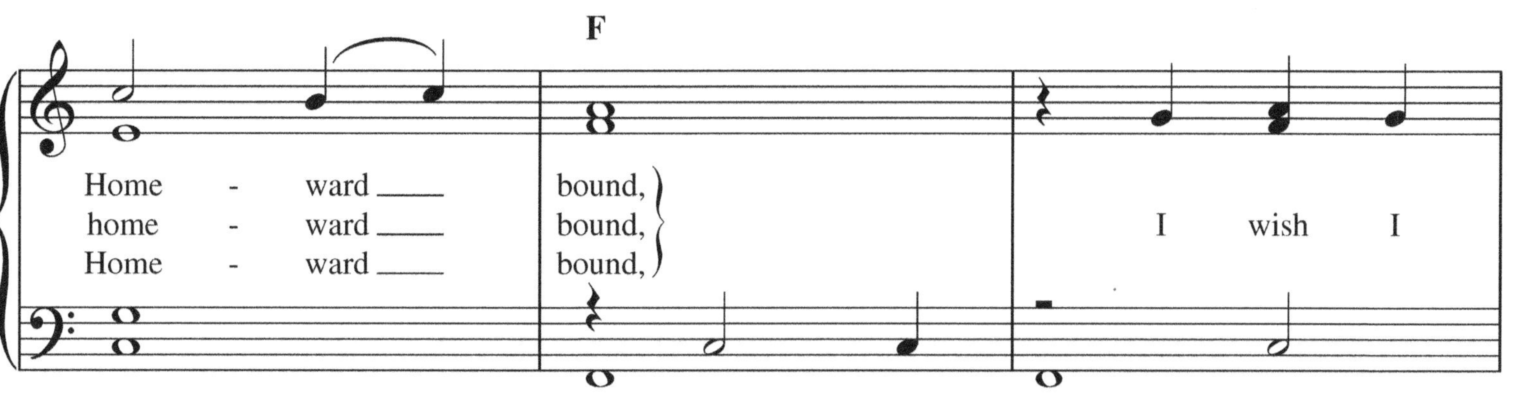

C
F
was
home - ward
bound.

C
Dm C B♭ F/A
3
1
Home, where my
thought's es - cap - ing,

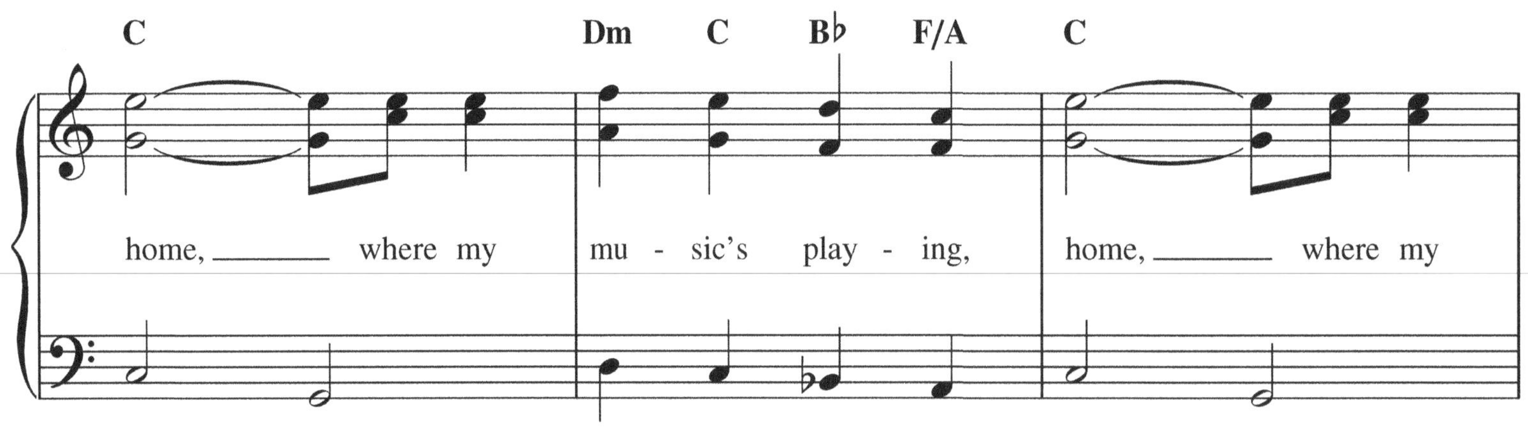
C
Dm C B♭ F/A
C
home, where my
mu - sic's play - ing,
home, where my

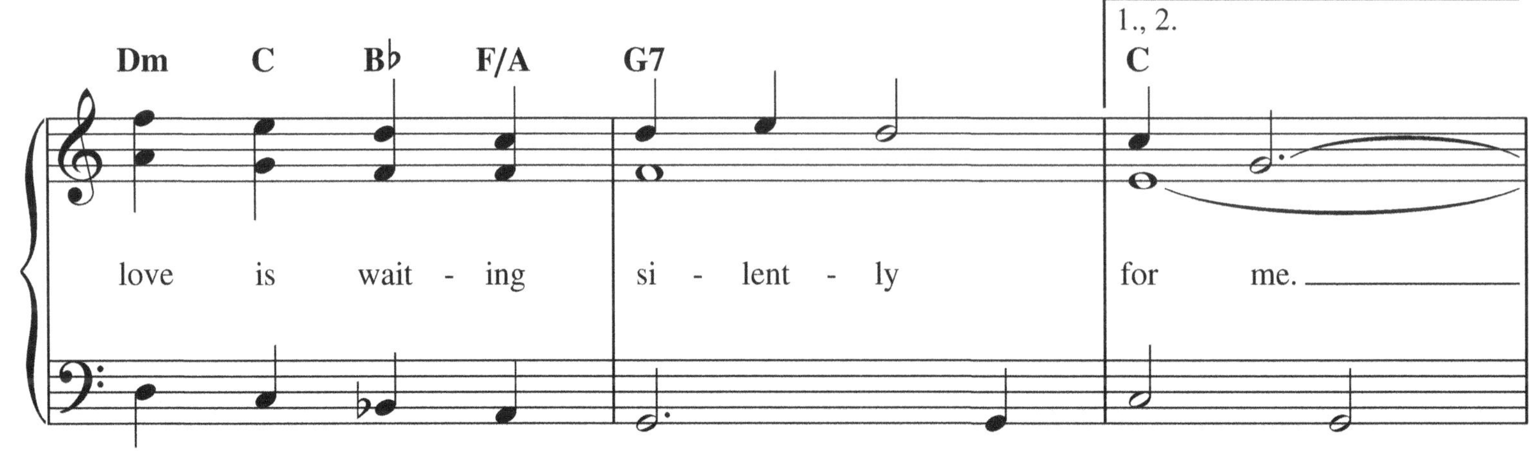
Dm C B♭ F/A
G7
1., 2.
C
love is wait - ing
si - lent - ly
for me.

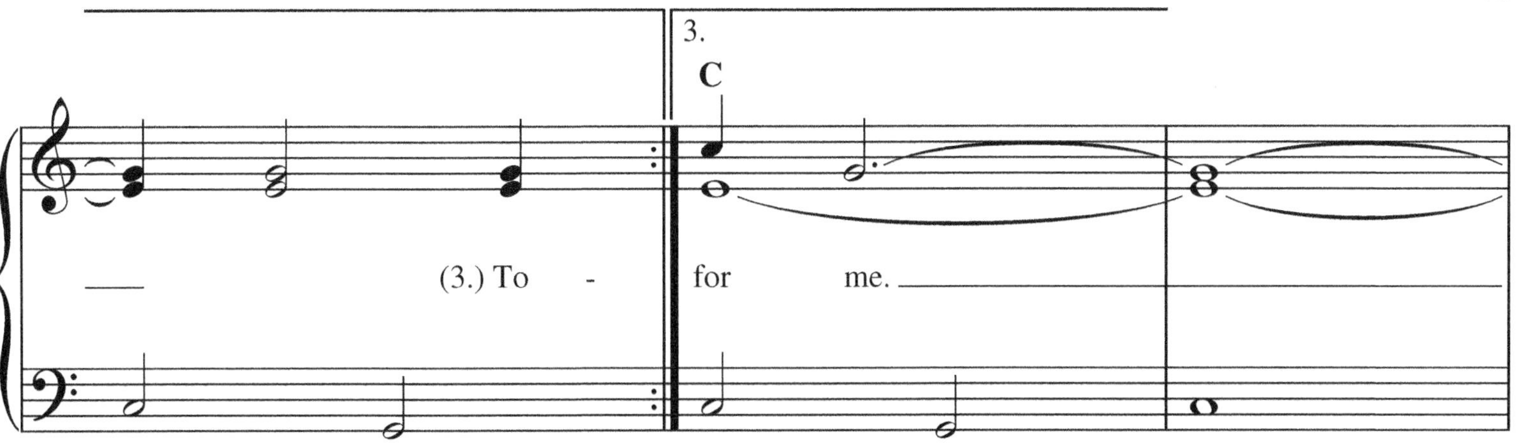
3.
C
(3.) To -
for me.

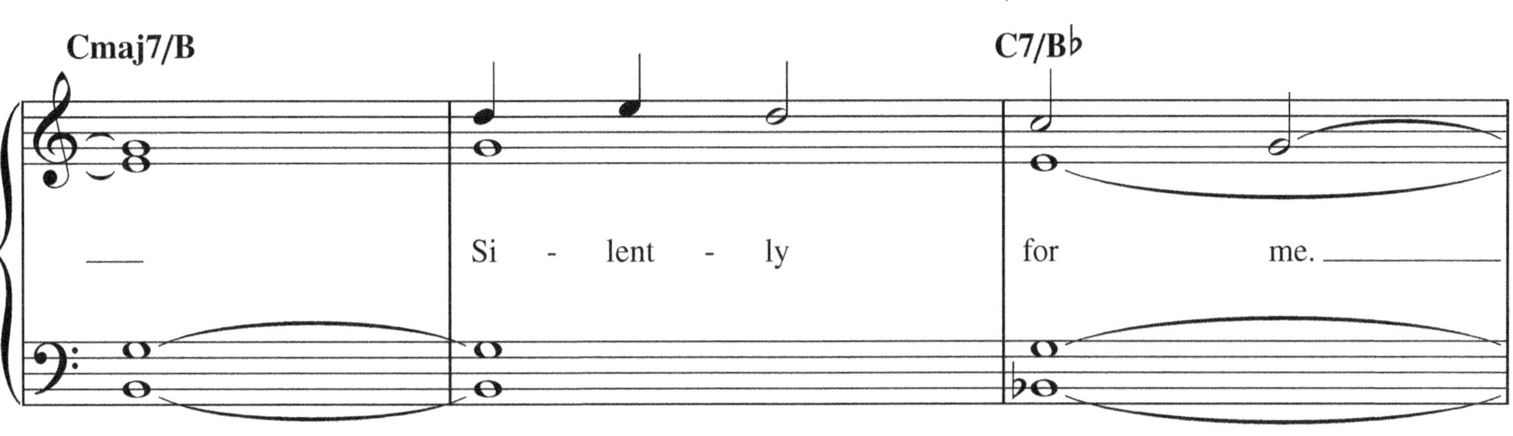
Cmaj7/B
C7/B♭
Si - lent - ly
for me.

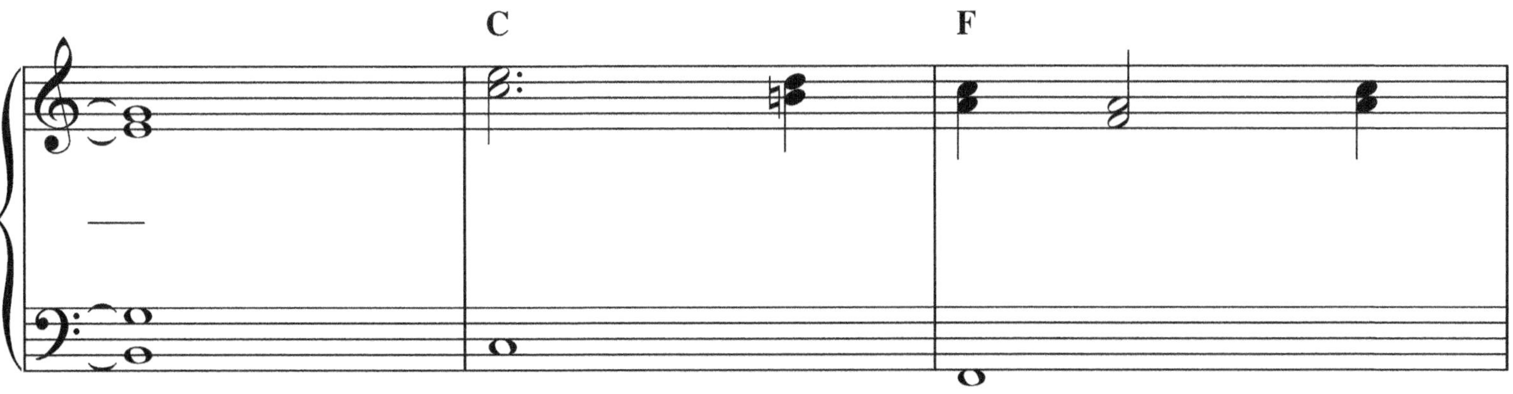
C
F

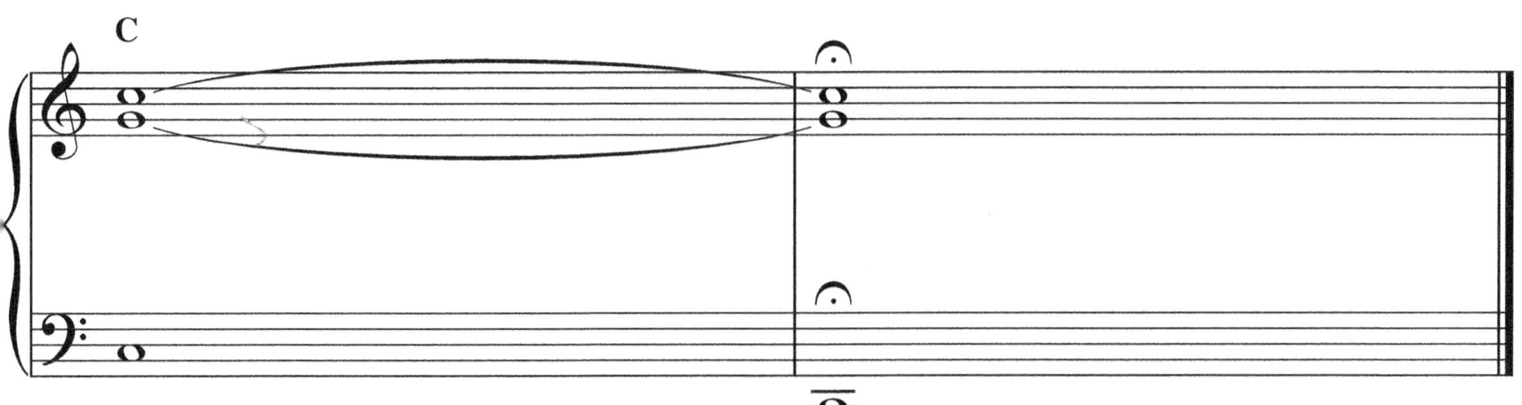
C

KODACHROME™

Words and Music by
PAUL SIMON

Am
D
G
it's a won - der
I can think at
all.

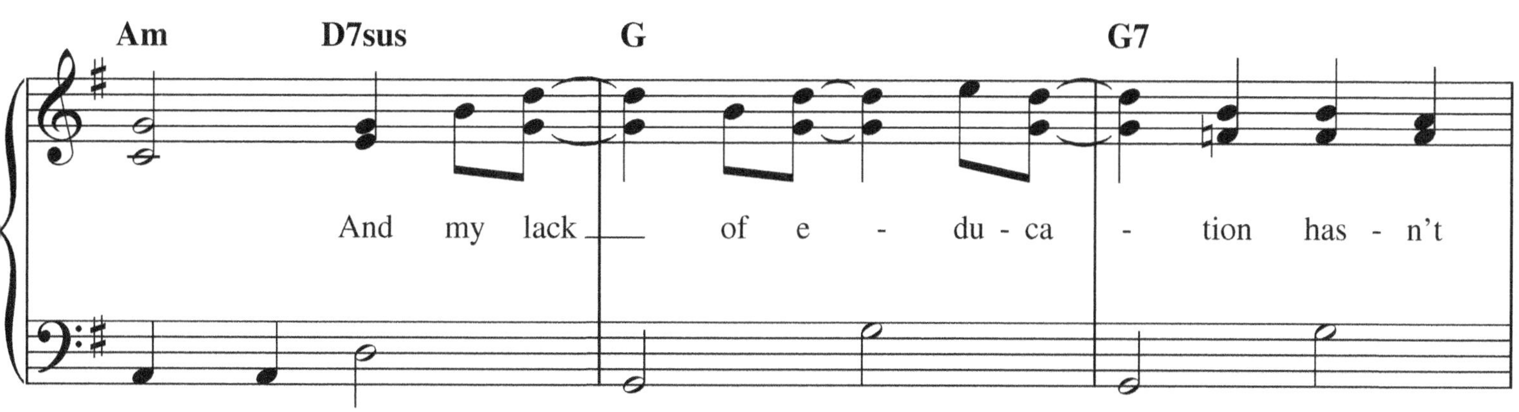
Am
D7sus
G
G7
And my lack of e - du - ca - tion has - n't

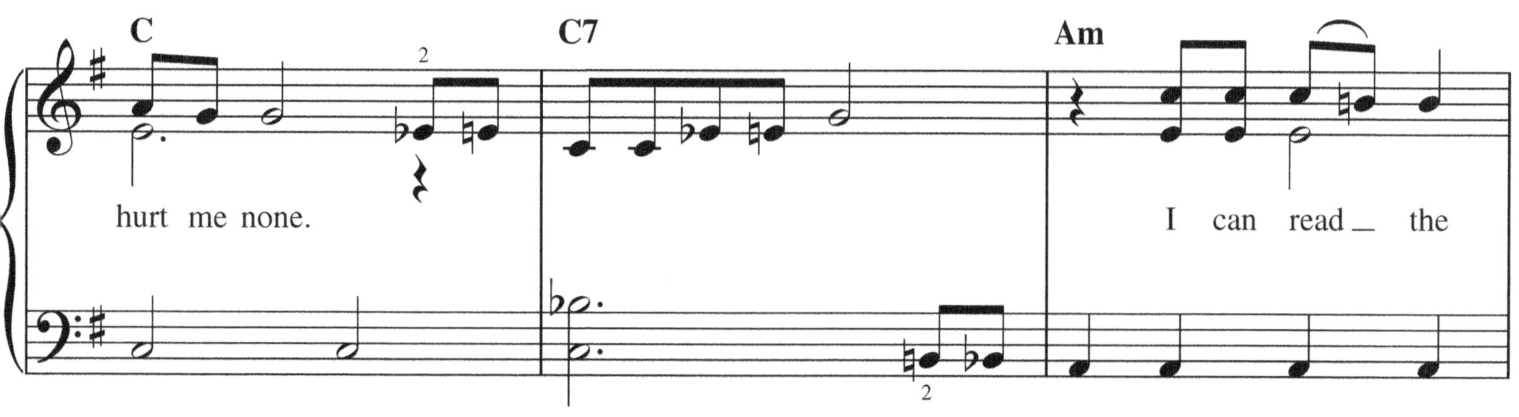
C
C7
Am
hurt me none.
I can read the

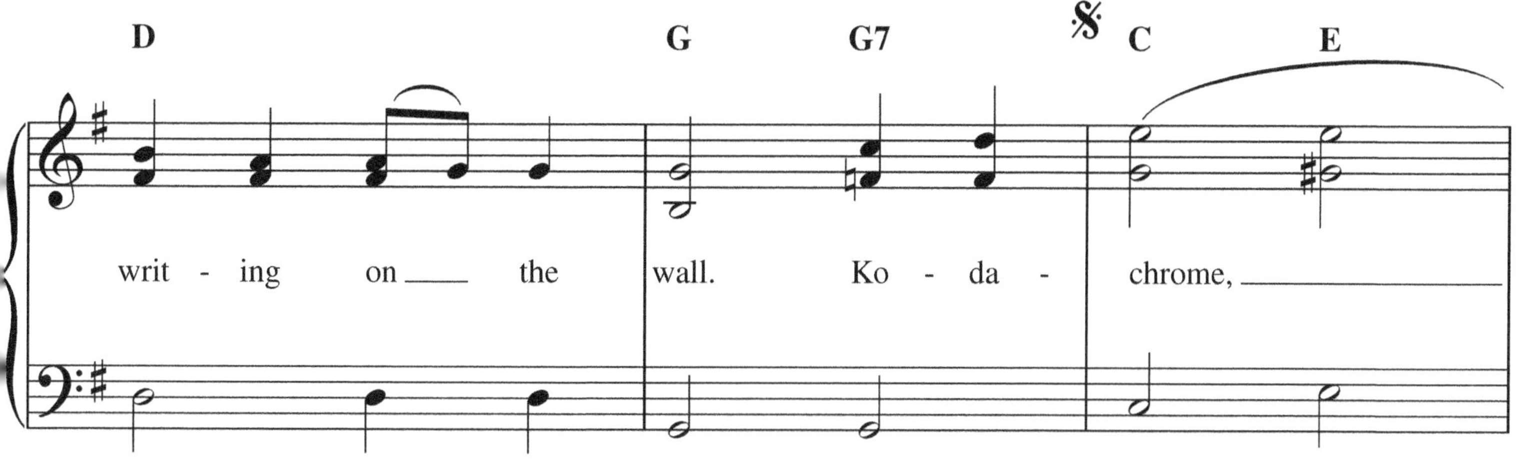
D
G
G7
C
E
writ - ing on the
wall.
Ko - da -
chrome,

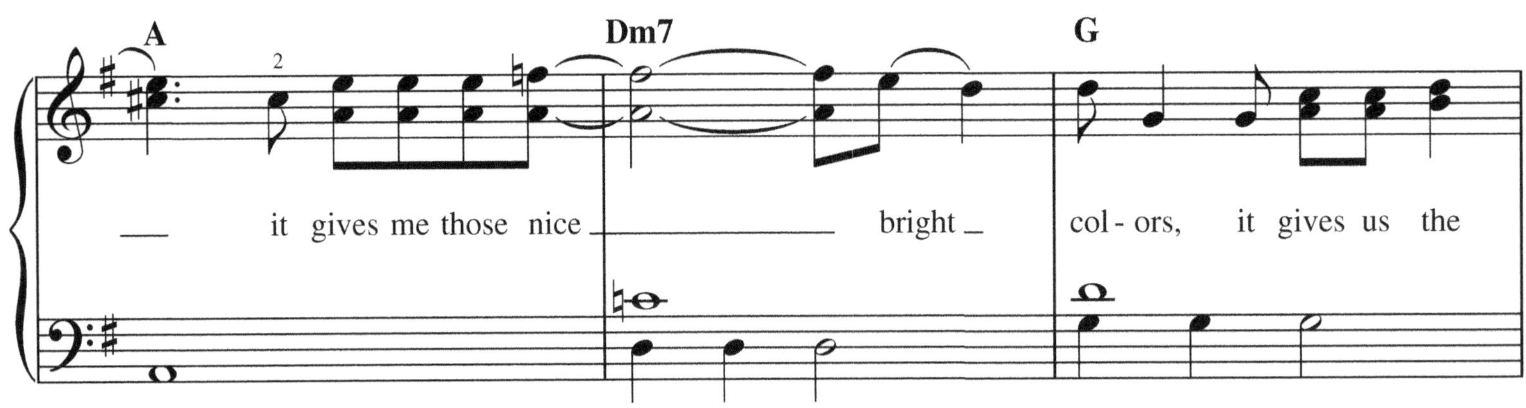
A
Dm7
G
2
it gives me those nice bright col - ors, it gives us the

C
F
D
greens of sum - mers, makes you think all the

G
C
E
A
world's a sun - ny day, oh yeah. I got a Ni -

Dm7
G
C
- kon cam - era, I love to take a pho - to - graph.

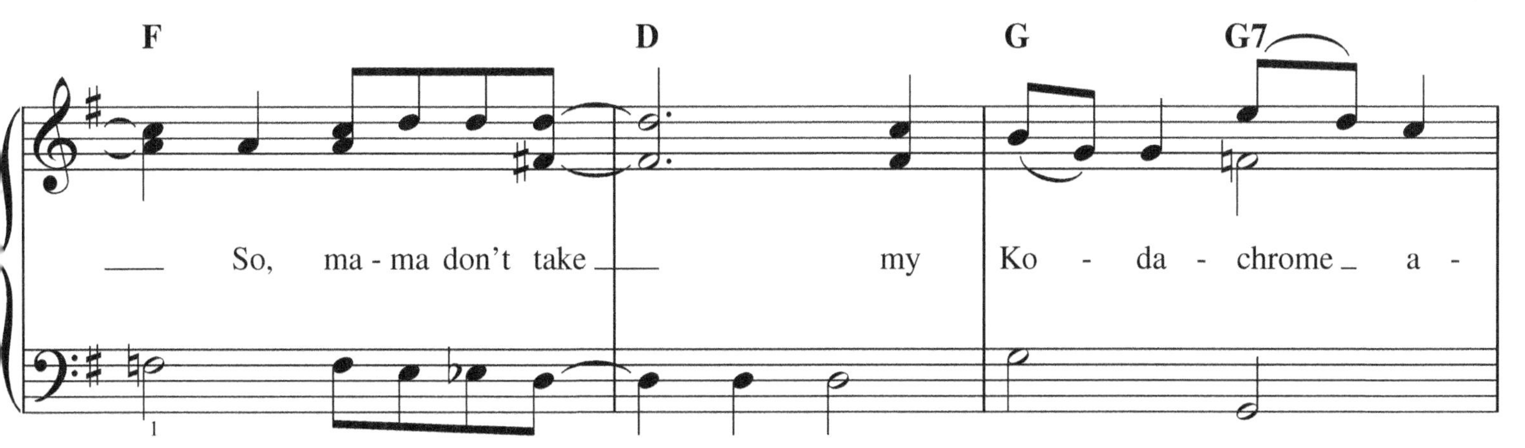
F
D
G
G7
So, ma - ma don't take my Ko - da - chrome a -

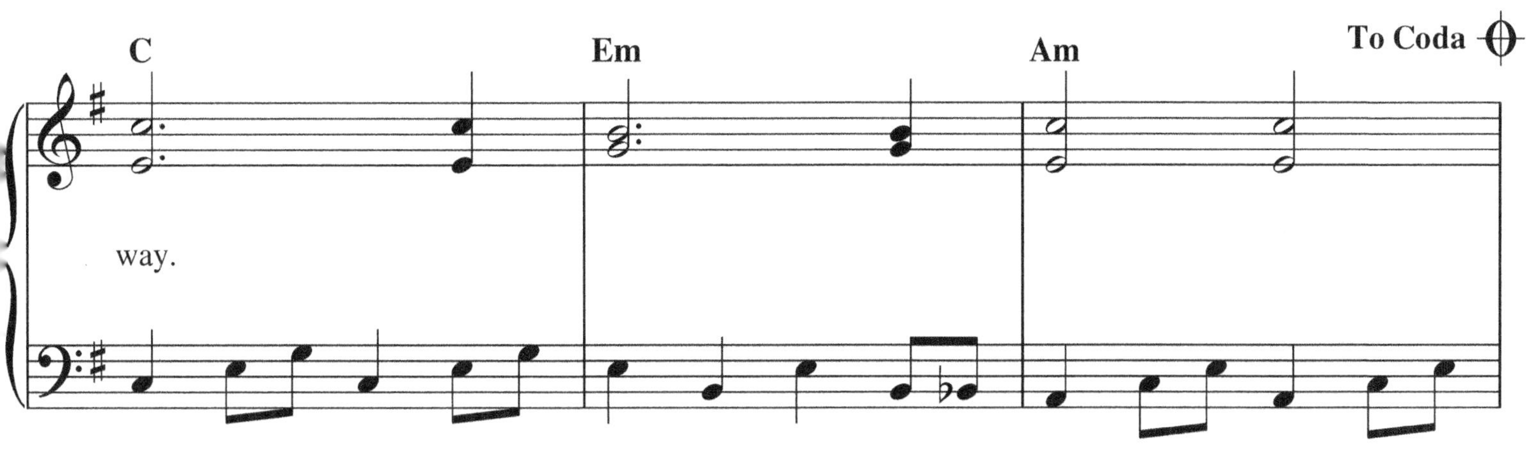
C
Em
Am
To Coda
way.

D
G
G7
If you took all the girls I knew when I was

C
C7
Am
sin - gle and brought 'em all to -

D
G
Am7
D7sus
geth - er for one night,
I know they'd

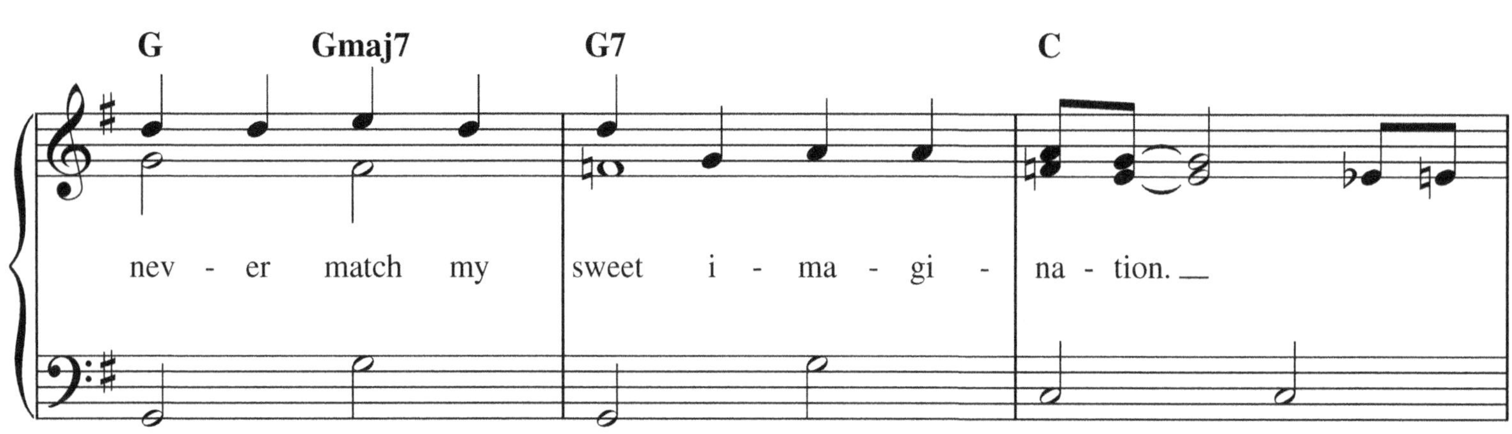
G
Gmaj7
G7
C
nev - er match my sweet i - ma - gi - na - tion.

C7
Am
G/D
D
And ev - 'ry - thing looks worse in black and

G
G7
D.S. al Coda
white. Ko - da -

CODA
Am
Ma - ma don't

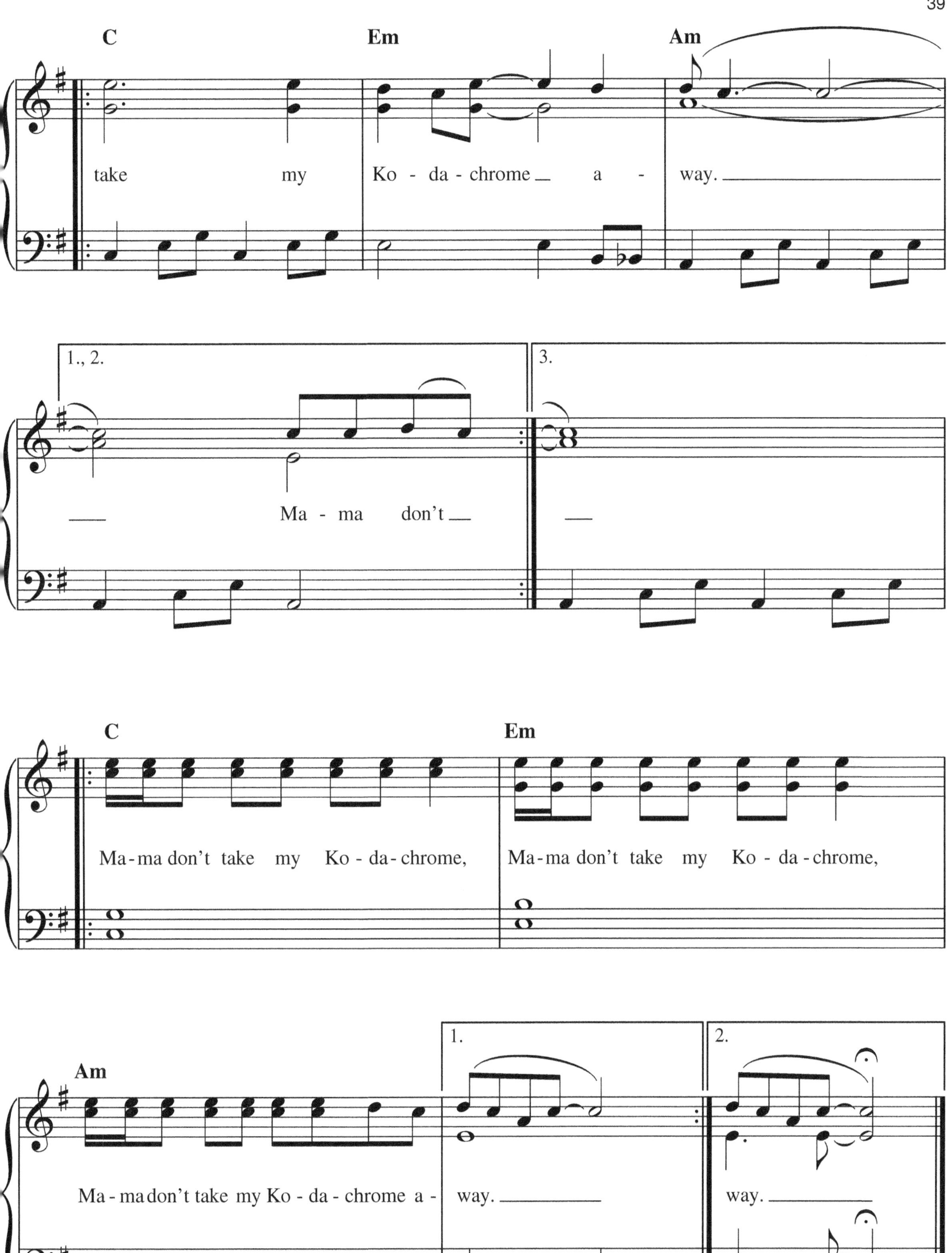
C
Em
Am
take my Ko - da - chrome a - way.
1., 2.
3.
Ma - ma don't
C
Em
Ma-ma don't take my Ko - da - chrome,
Ma-ma don't take my Ko - da - chrome,
Am
1.
2.
Ma - ma don't take my Ko - da - chrome a - way.
way.

ME AND JULIO DOWN BY THE SCHOOLYARD

Words and Music by
PAUL SIMON

G
start - ed the in - ves - ti - ga - tion. It's a - gainst the
D
G
law, it was a-gainst the law, oh, what the Ma - ma
D
G C/G G
saw, it was a - gainst the law. Ooh,
G
Ma - ma looked down and spit on the ground ev - 'ry time my name gets
D.S. (See additional lyrics)

C
D
men - tioned.
Pa - pa said, "Oi, if I get that boy I'm gon - na

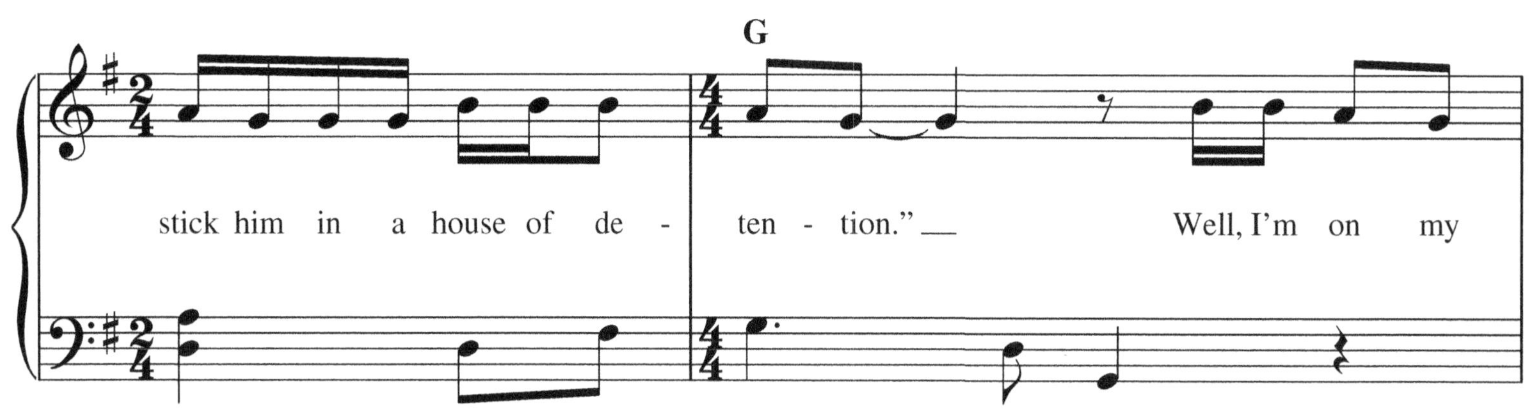
G
stick him in a house of de -
ten - tion."
Well, I'm on my

C
G
way,
I don't know
where I'm go - in'.
I'm on my

C
G
A7
D
way.
I'm tak - in' my
time but I don't know where. Good - bye to

C F G
Ros - y, the Queen of Co - ro - na. See
F C D G C G
To Coda
me and Ju - li - o down by the school - yard. See
F C D G C G D
me and Ju - li - o down by the school - yard.
D.S. al Coda
Whoa, in a
CODA
F C D
me and Ju - li - o down by the school - yard.

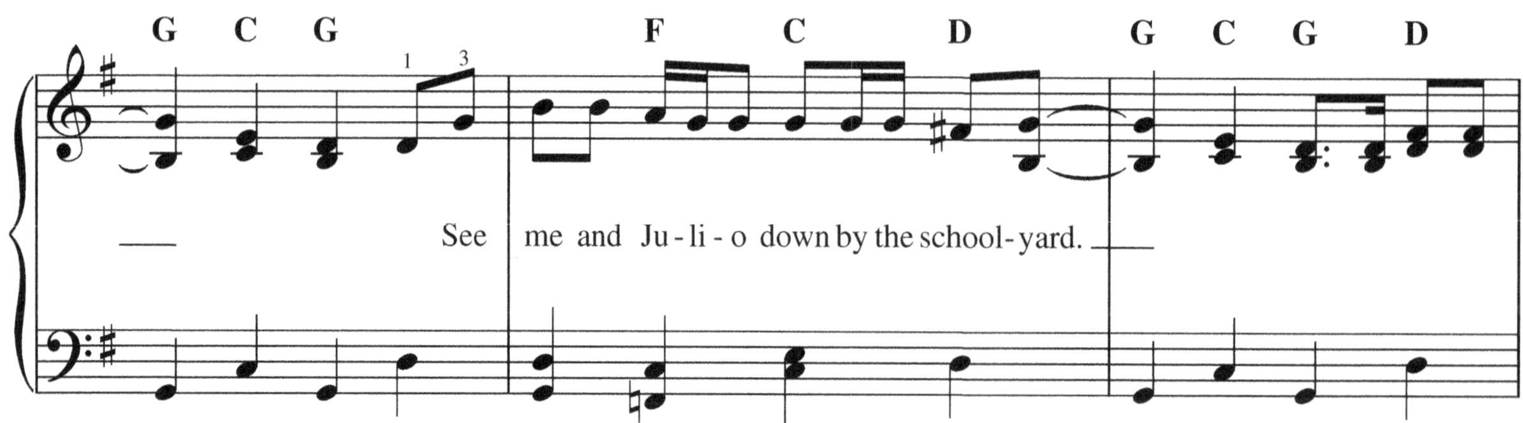

Additional Lyrics

In a couple of days they come and take me away
But the press let their story leak.
And when the radical Priest come to get me released
We was all on the cover of *Newsweek.*

And I'm on my way *etc.*

MRS. ROBINSON

Words and Music by
PAUL SIMON

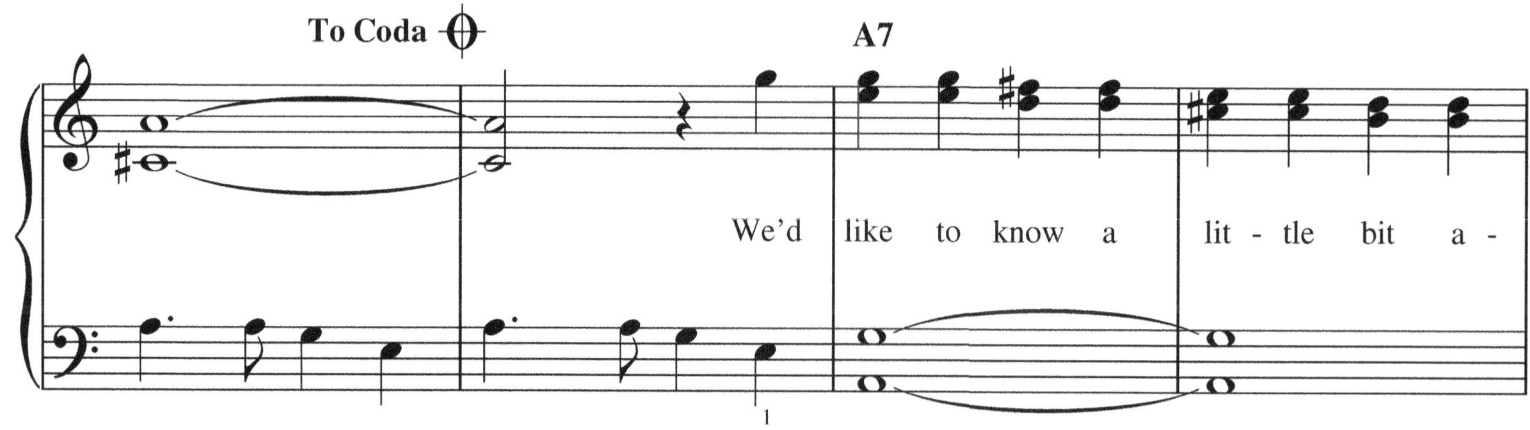
To Coda
A7
We'd like to know a lit - tle bit a -
1

D7
bout you for our files. We'd like to help you

G7
learn to help your - self. Look a-round you,

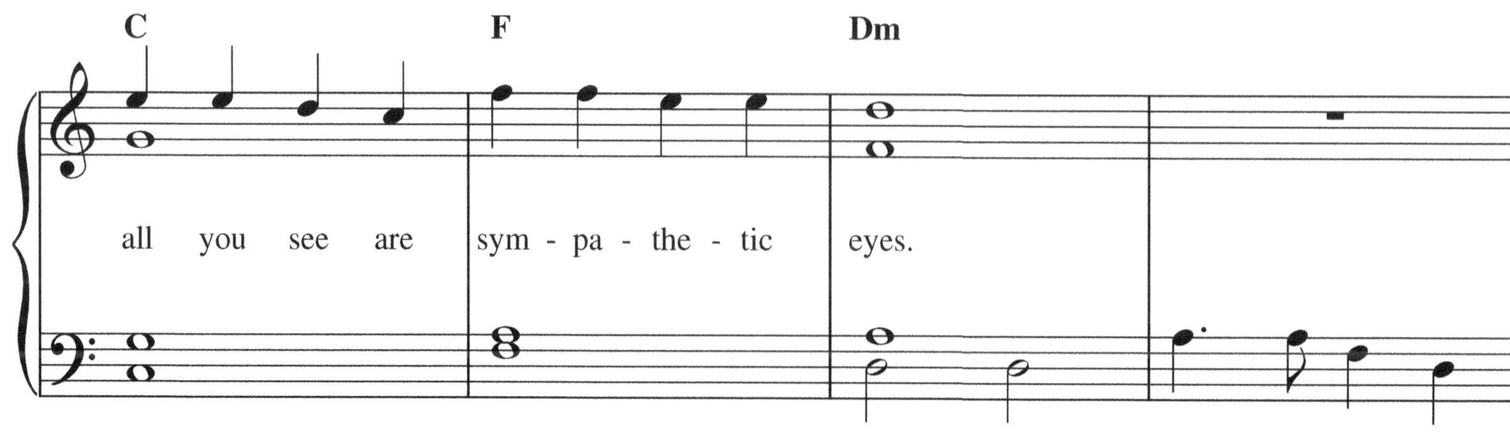
C
F
Dm
all you see are sym - pa - the - tic eyes.

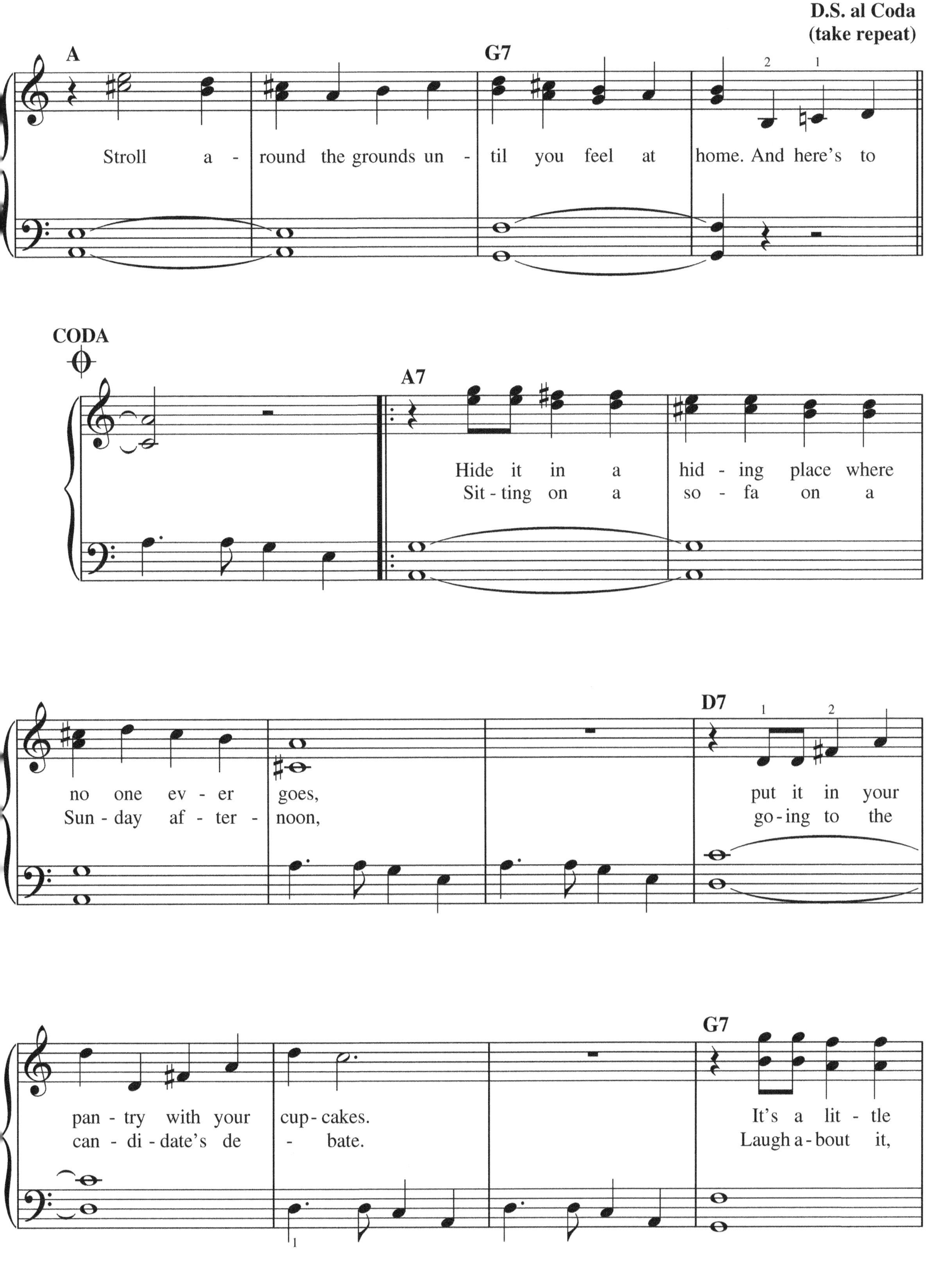

D.S. al Coda
(take repeat)

A G7

Stroll a - round the grounds un - til you feel at home. And here's to

CODA

A7

Hide it in a hid - ing place where
Sit - ting on a so - fa on a

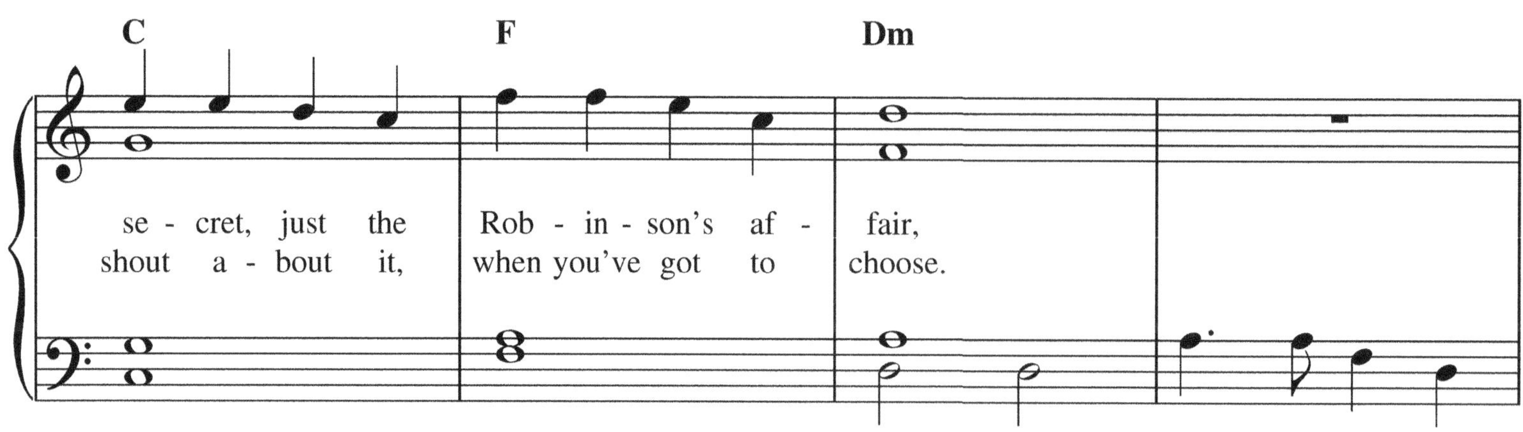
C
F
Dm
se - cret, just the
shout a - bout it,
Rob - in - son's af -
when you've got to
fair,
choose.

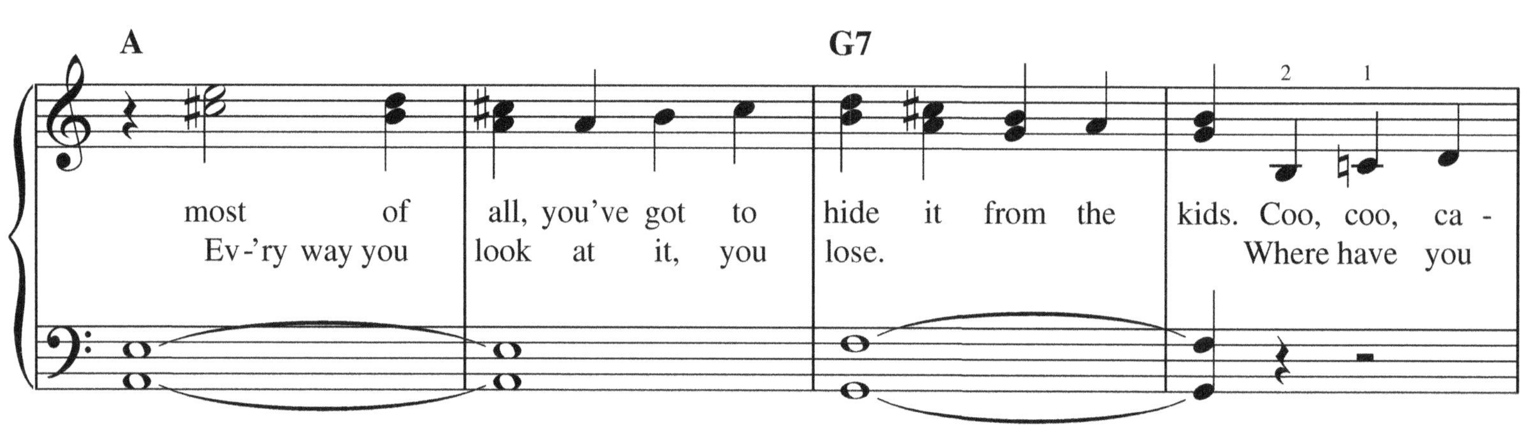
A
G7
most of
Ev-'ry way you
all, you've got to
look at it, you
hide it from the
lose.
kids. Coo, coo, ca -
Where have you

C
Am
C
choo, Mrs.
gone, Joe Di -
Rob - in - son,
Mag - gi - o? A
Je - sus loves you
na - tion turns its

Am
F
G7
more than you will
lone - ly eyes to
know.
you.
(Wo, wo,
(Woo woo,
wo.)
woo.)

C
Am
2
1
God bless you, please, Mrs. Rob - in - son,
What's that you say, Mrs. Rob - in - son,

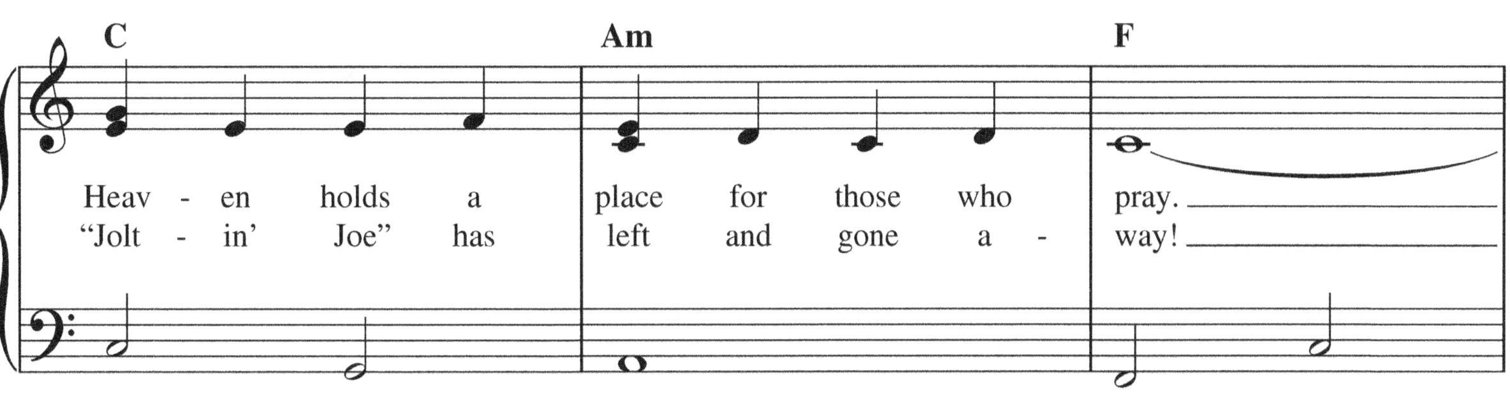
C
Am
F
Heav - en holds a place for those who pray.
"Jolt - in' Joe" has left and gone a - way!

Dm
A
(Hey, hey, hey. hey, hey, hey.)
(Hey, hey, hey. hey, hey, hey.)

1.
2.

SLIP SLIDIN' AWAY

Words and Music by
PAUL SIMON

G
D
C
D
G
C/G
near - er your des - ti - na - tion, the more you're slip slid - in' a - way.
G
Em
I know a man,
- an;
he came from
be-came a
G
C
D
my home town.
wife.
He wore his
These are the
pas - sion for his wom - an like a
ver - y words she us - es to de -
tell him all the rea - sons for the
C
C9
G
thorn - y crown.
scribe her life.
things he'd done.
He said, "De -
She said, "A
He came a
lor - es,
good day
long way

D/F#
Em
Em7
I live in fear. My love for
ain't got no rain." She said, "A
just to ex - plain. He kissed his
G
D
C6
D
you's so ov - er - pow'r - ing I'm a - fraid that I will dis - ap -
bad day's when I lie in bed and think of things that might have
boy as he lay sleep - ing then he turned a - round and head - ed home a -
G
pear."
been."
gain.
Slip slid - in' a - way.
D/F#
Em
3
Slip slid - in' a - way.
You know the

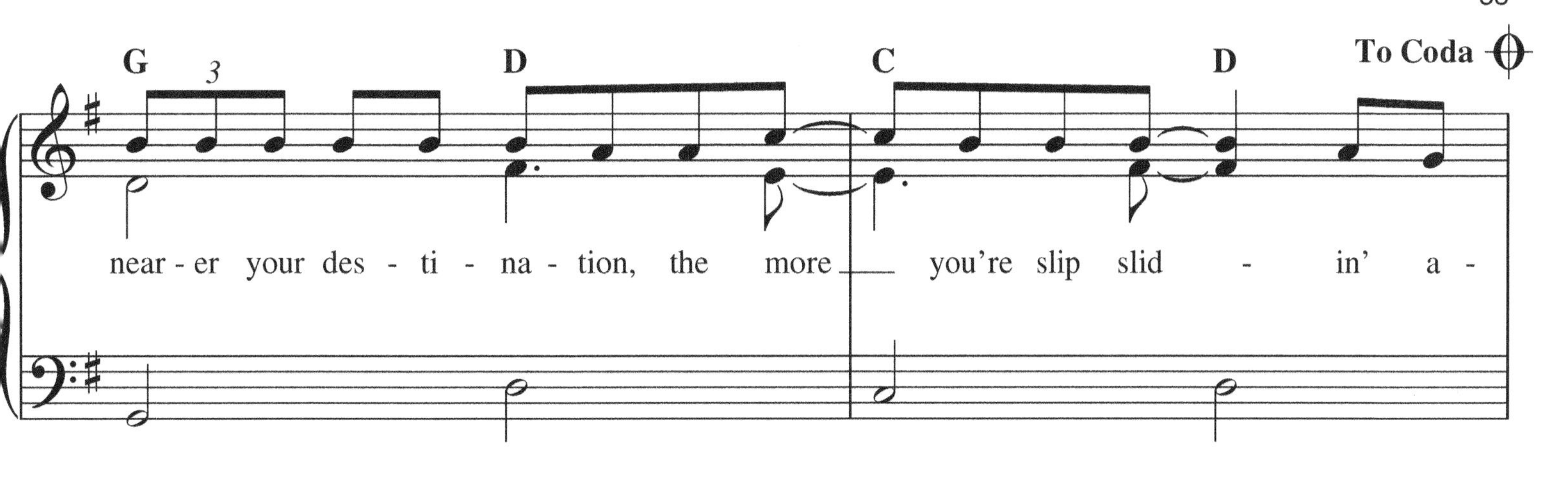
G D C D
To Coda
3
near - er your des - ti - na - tion, the more you're slip slid - in' a -

1.
Gsus G C/G G
2.
Gsus G F
way. I know a wom - way.

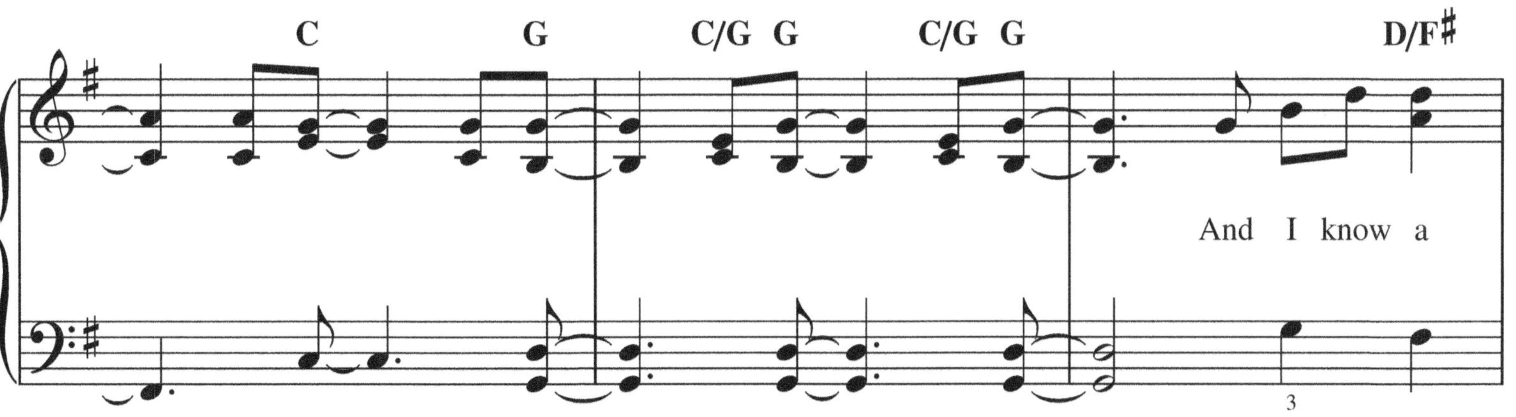
C G C/G G C/G G D/F♯
And I know a
3

C/E D G
D.S. al Coda
fa - ther who had a son. He longed to

CODA
Gsus G F
way.

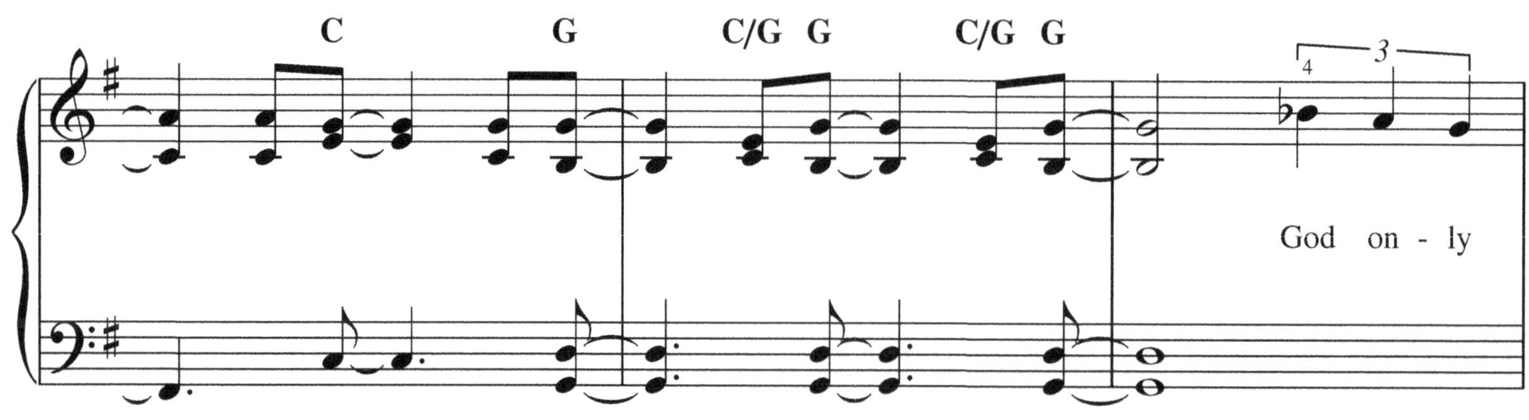
C
G
C/G G
C/G G
God on - ly

Em
G
knows.
God makes His
plan.

C
D
C
The in - for - ma - tion's un - a - vail - a - ble to the mor - tal man.

C9
G
D/F♯
We're work - in' our jobs;
col - lect our

Em
Em7
G
D
pay;
be-lieve we're
glid-in' down the high-way, when in
C6
D
G
C/G
G
fact, we're slip slid-in' a-way.
Slip slid-in' a-
C/G
G
D/F♯
Em
way.
Slip slid-in' a-way.
G
D
You know the
near-er your des-ti-na-tion, the more

1.
C
D
G
C/G
G
you're slip slid - in' a - way.
Slip slid - in' a -
2.
G
C/G
G
G
way.
Bm/F♯
1.
Em
2.
Em
D/F♯
G

YOU CAN CALL ME AL

Words and Music by
PAUL SIMON

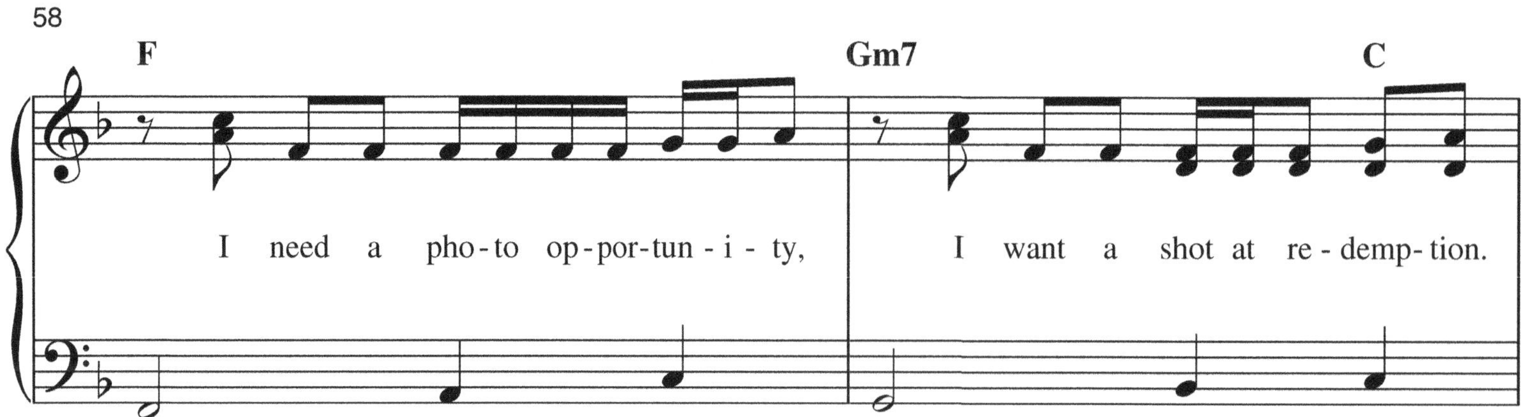
F
Gm7
C
I need a pho-to op-por-tun-i-ty,
I want a shot at re-demp-tion.

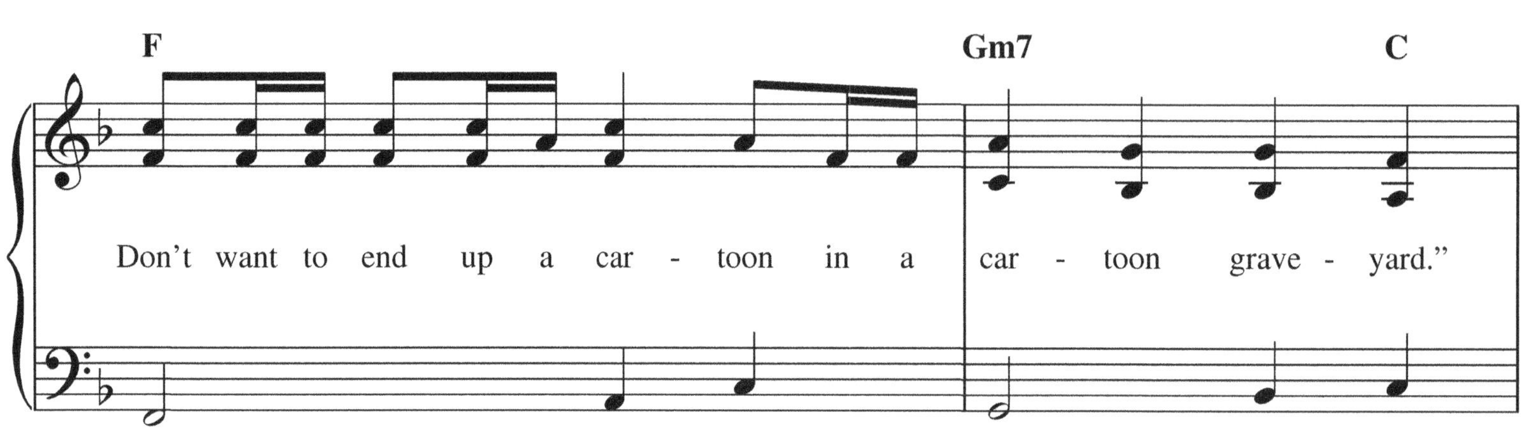
F
Gm7
C
Don't want to end up a car - toon in a
car - toon grave - yard."

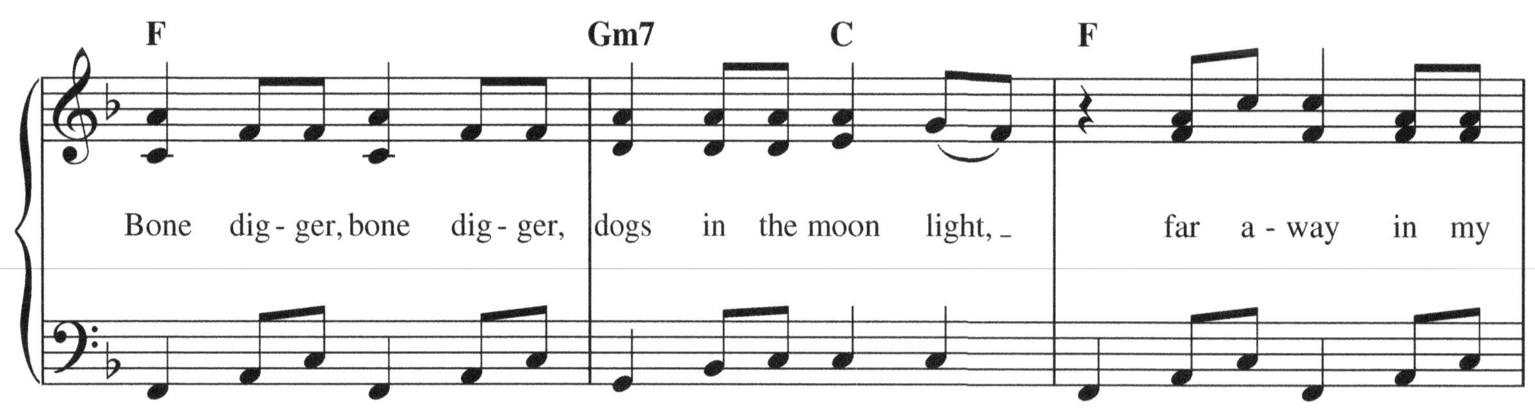
F
Gm7
C
F
Bone dig-ger, bone dig-ger,
dogs in the moon light,
far a-way in my

Gm7
C
F
Gm7
C
well-lit door.
Mis-ter
beer bel-ly, beer bel-ly,
get these mutts a-way from me.

F
Gm7
N.C.
F
C
I don't find this stuff a - mus - ing an - y - more.
If you'll be my bod - y - guard

Gm7
C
F
Gm7
C
I can be your long _ lost pal.

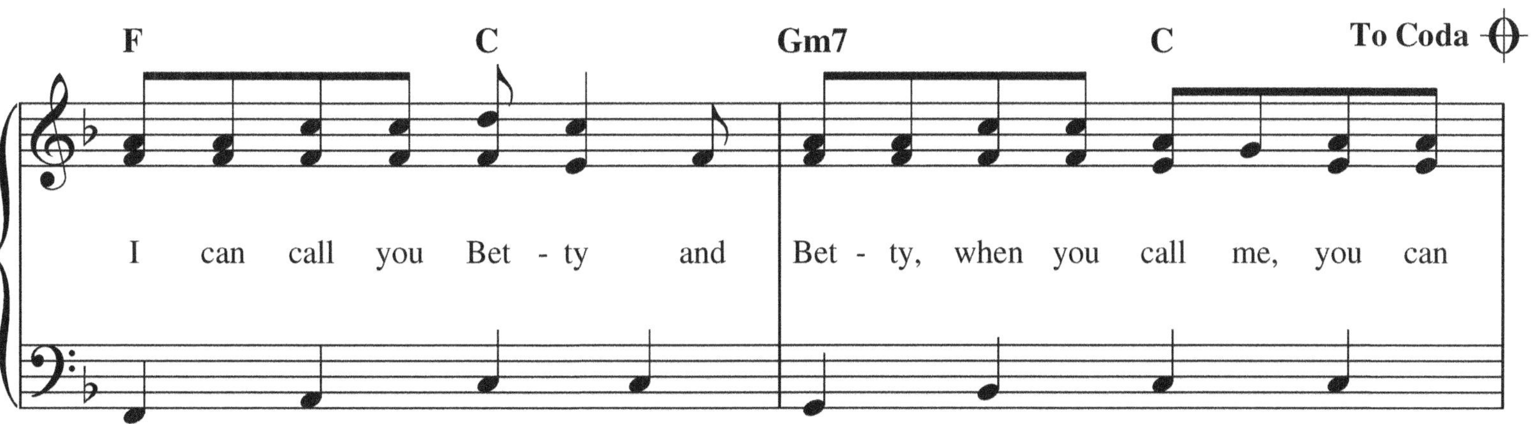
F
C
Gm7
C
To Coda
I can call you Bet - ty and Bet - ty, when you call me, you can

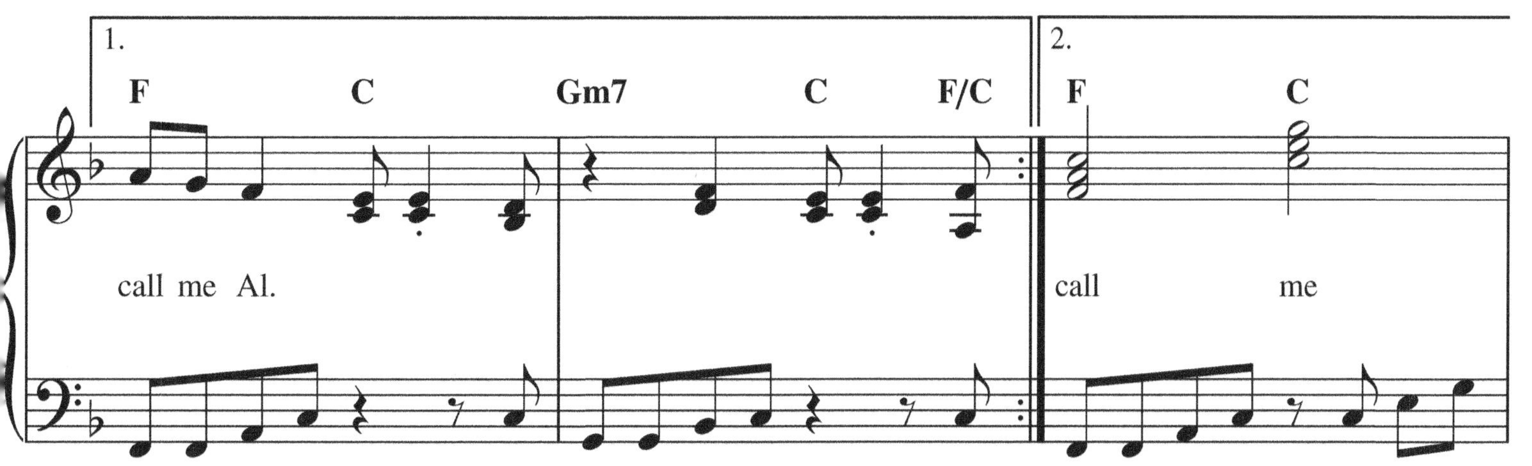
1.
F
C
Gm7
C
F/C
2.
F
C
call me Al.
call me

Gm7
F
C
Gm7
C
F/C
Al.
Call
me
Al.

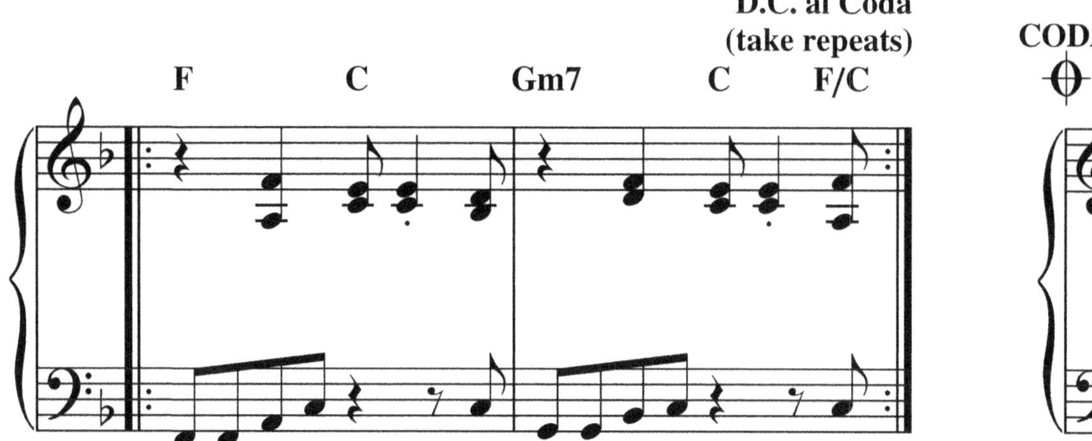
D.C. al Coda
(take repeats)
F
C
Gm7
C
F/C

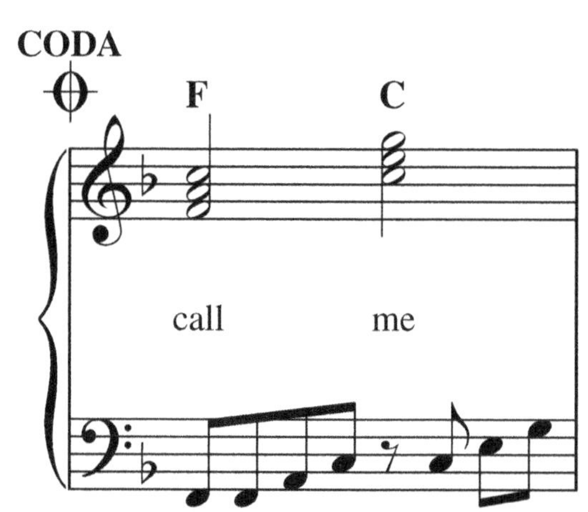
CODA
F
C
call
me

Gm7
C
F
Gm7
C
Al.
Call
me.
Na
na
na
na
na
na
na
na.

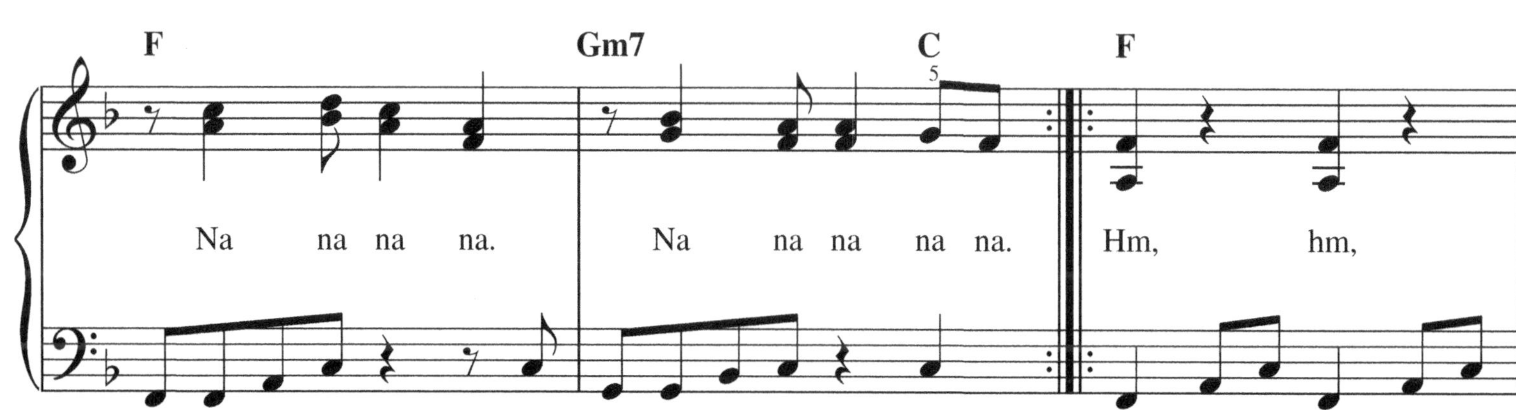
F
Gm7
C
F
Na
na
na
na.
Na
na
na
na
na.
Hm,
hm,

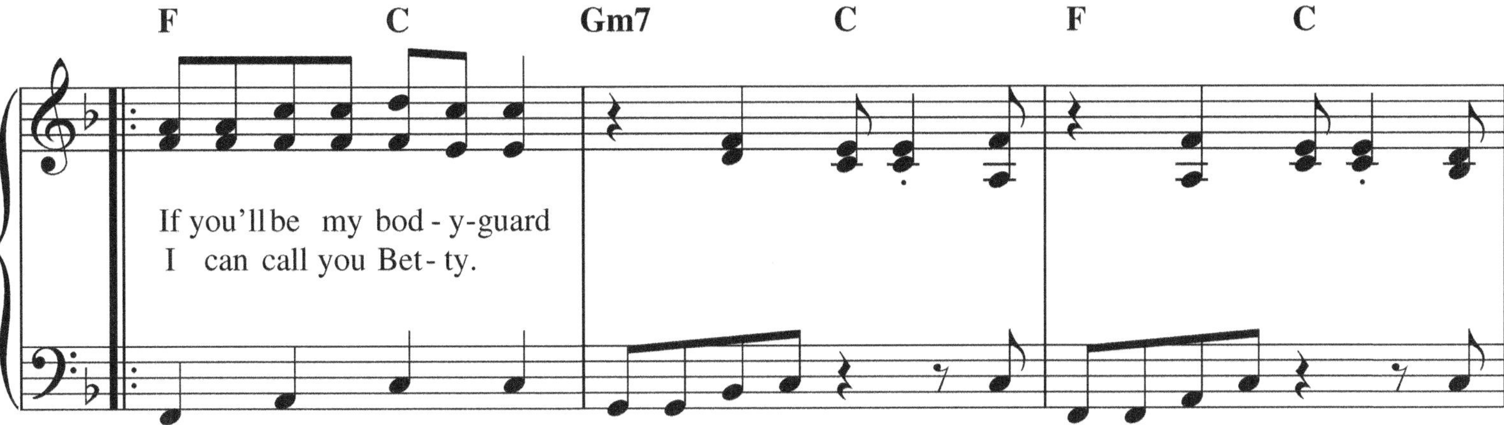

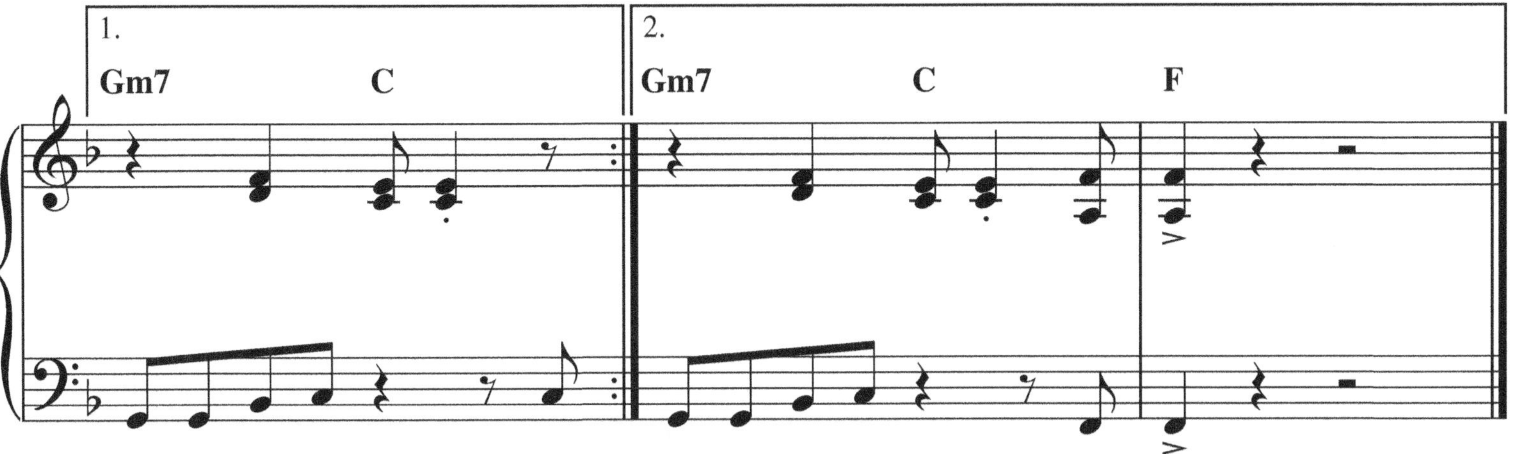

Additional Lyrics

2. A man walks down the street, he says,
"Why am I so short of attention?
Got a short little span of attention
And oh, my nights are so long.
Where's my wife and family?
What if I die here?
Who'll be my role model
Now that my role model is gone, gone?"
He ducked back down the alley with some
Roly-poly little bat-faced girl.
All along, along, there were incidents and accidents.
There were hints and allegations.

If you'll be my bodyguard....

3. A man walks down the street, it's a
Street in a strange world.
Maybe it's the third world.
Maybe his first time around.
Doesn't speak the language.
He holds no currency. He is a foreign man.
He is surrounded by the sound, the sound;
Cattle in the marketplace,
Scatterings of orphanages.
He looks around, around.
He sees angels in the architecture
Spinning in infinity. He says amen and hallelujah.

If you'll be my bodyguard....

THE SOUND OF SILENCE

Words and Music by
PAUL SIMON

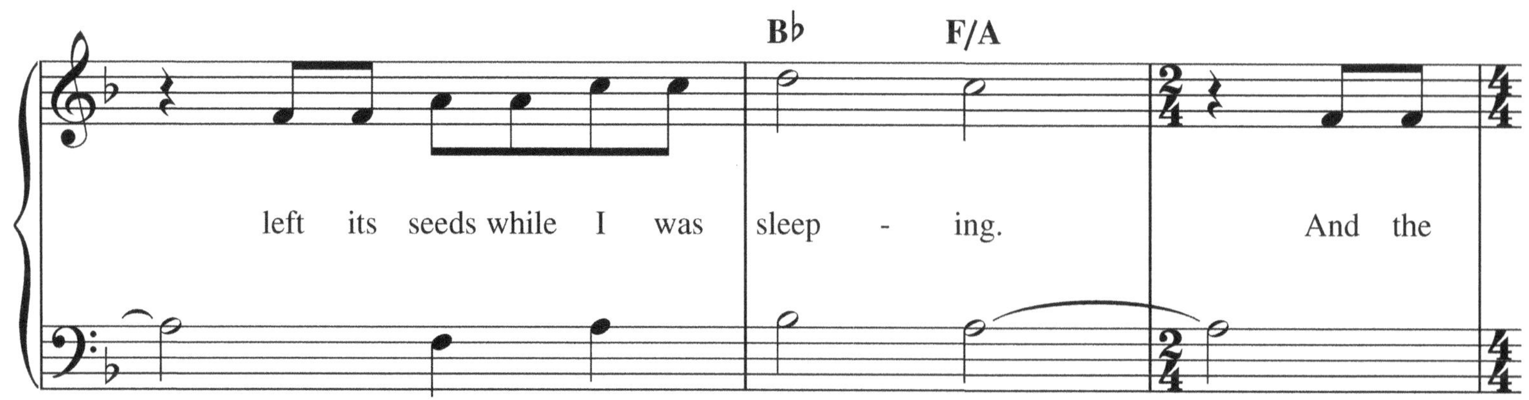

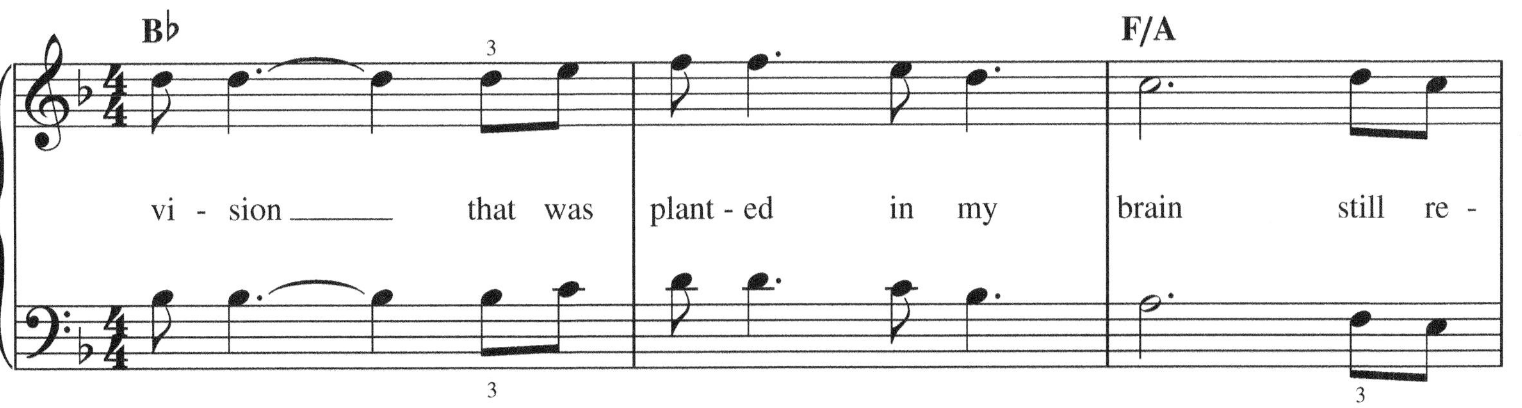
B♭
F/A
vi - sion ___ that was plant - ed in my brain still re -

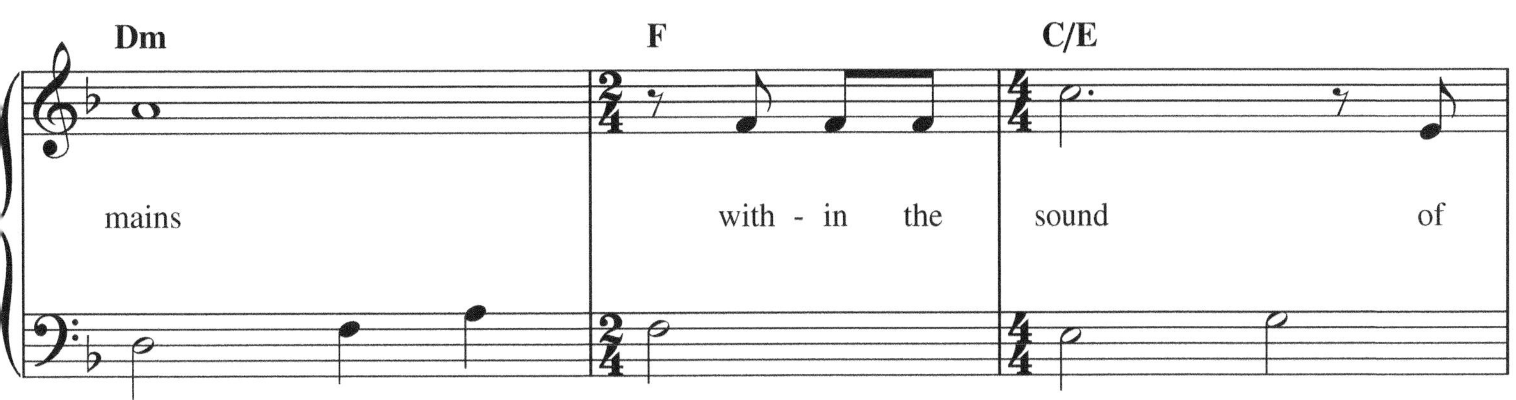
Dm
F
C/E
mains with - in the sound of

Dm
C
si - lence. ___
mp
In rest - less dreams I walked a - lone;
And in the na - ked light I saw

Dm
nar - row streets of cob - ble - stone, 'neath the ha - lo of a
ten thou - sand peo - ple, may - be more. Peo - ple talk - ing with - out

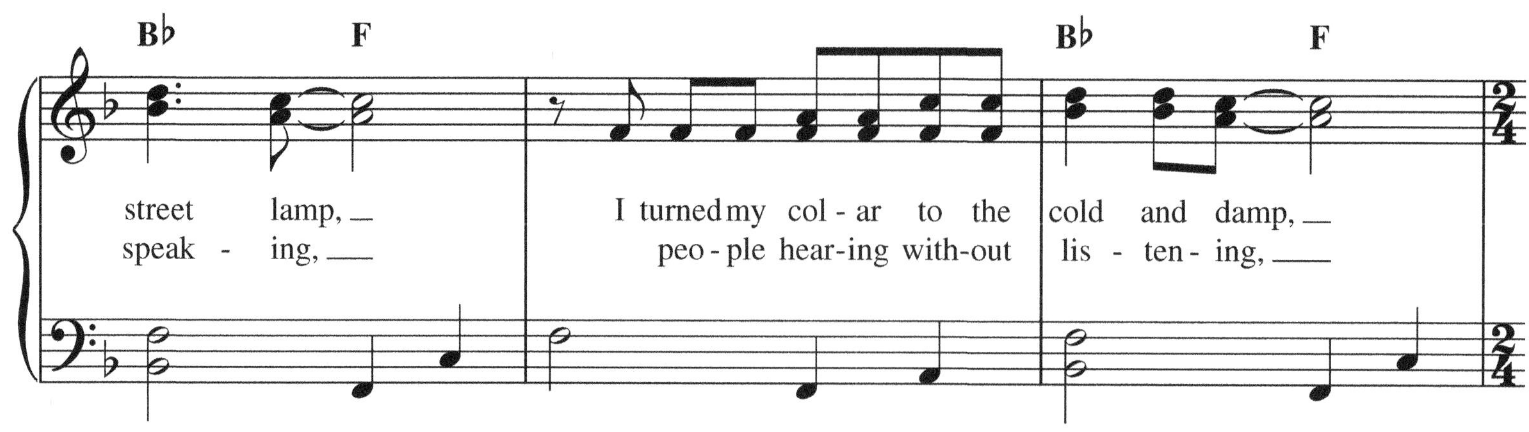
B♭
F
B♭
F
street lamp, _
I turned my col - ar to the
cold and damp, _
speak - ing, _
peo - ple hear-ing with-out
lis - ten - ing, _

B♭
when my
eyes were stabbed _ by the
flash of a ne - on
peo - ple
writ - ing songs _ that
voic - es _ nev - er

F
Dm
F
light that split the
night
and touched the
share, and no one
dare
dis - turb the

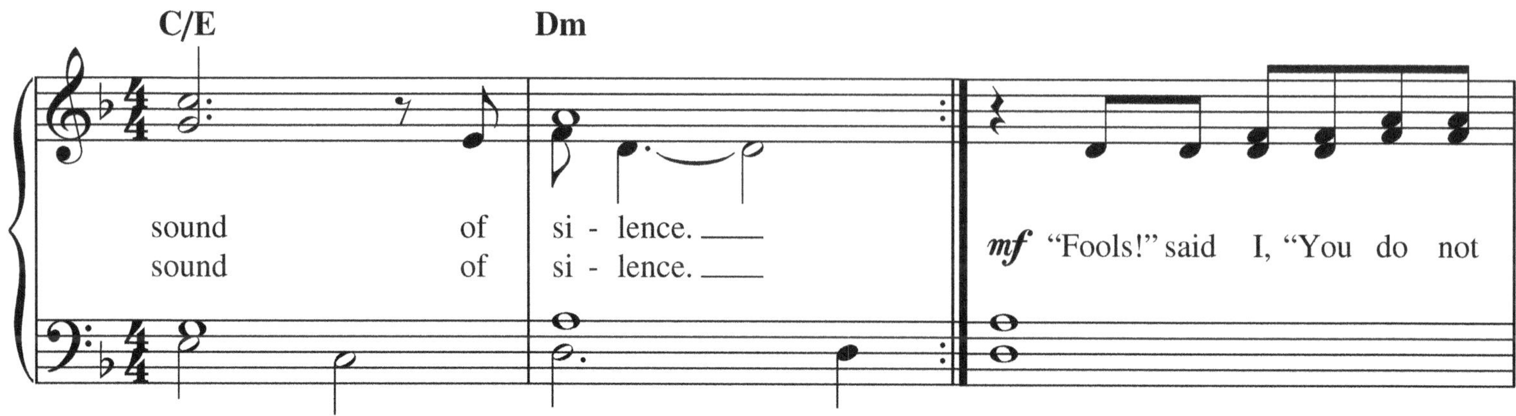
C/E
Dm
sound of
si - lence. _
sound of
si - lence. _
mf "Fools!" said I, "You do not

C/E
Dm
know
si - lence like a can - cer grows.

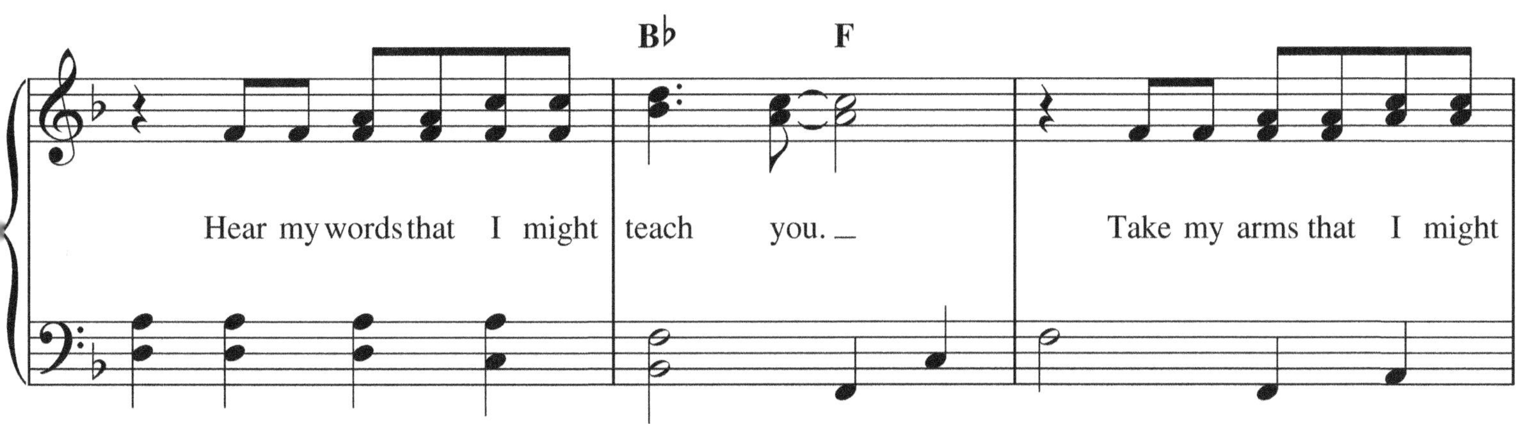
B♭
F
Hear my words that I might teach you. _
Take my arms that I might

B♭
F
B♭
reach you." _
But my words like

F
Dm
si - lent rain - drops fell,
and

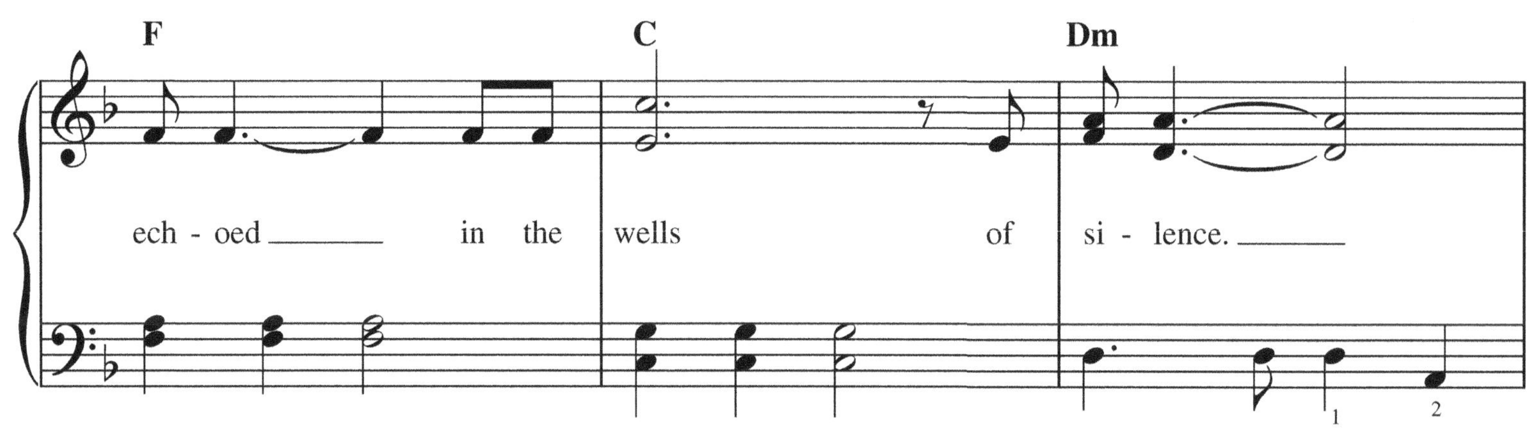
F
C
Dm
ech - oed ____ in the wells of si - lence. ____
1
2

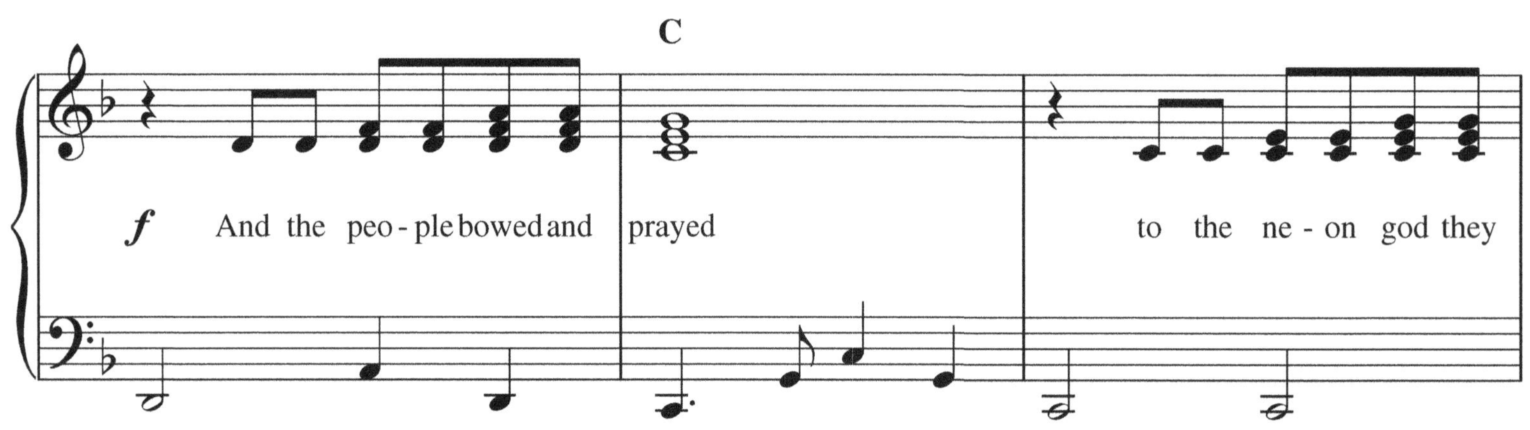
C
f
And the peo - ple bowed and prayed to the ne - on god they

Dm
B♭
F
made. And the sign flashed out its warn - ing __

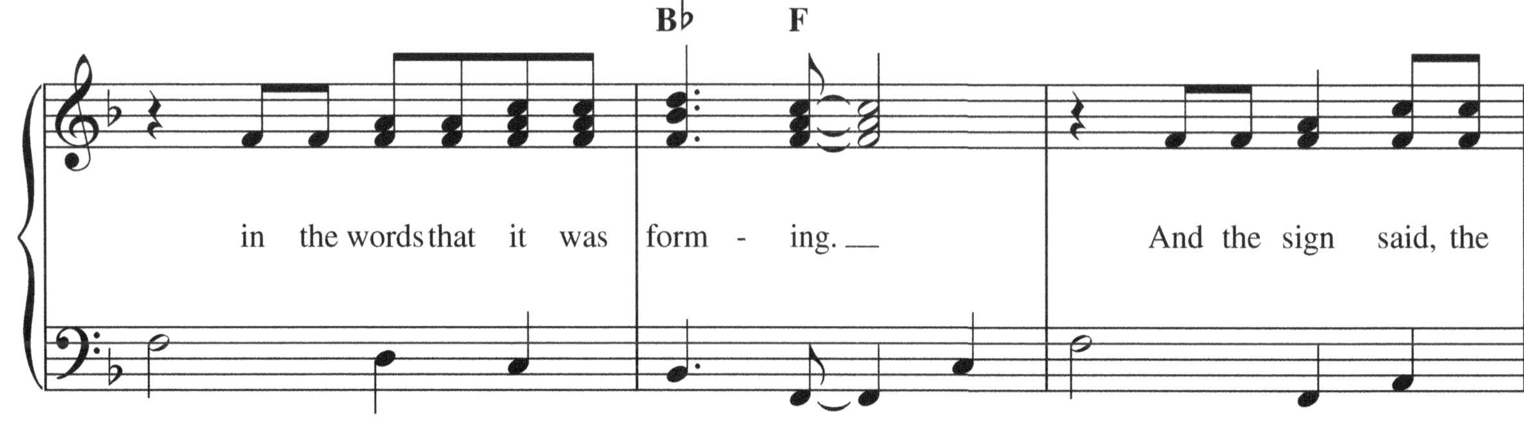
B♭
F
in the words that it was form - ing. __ And the sign said, the

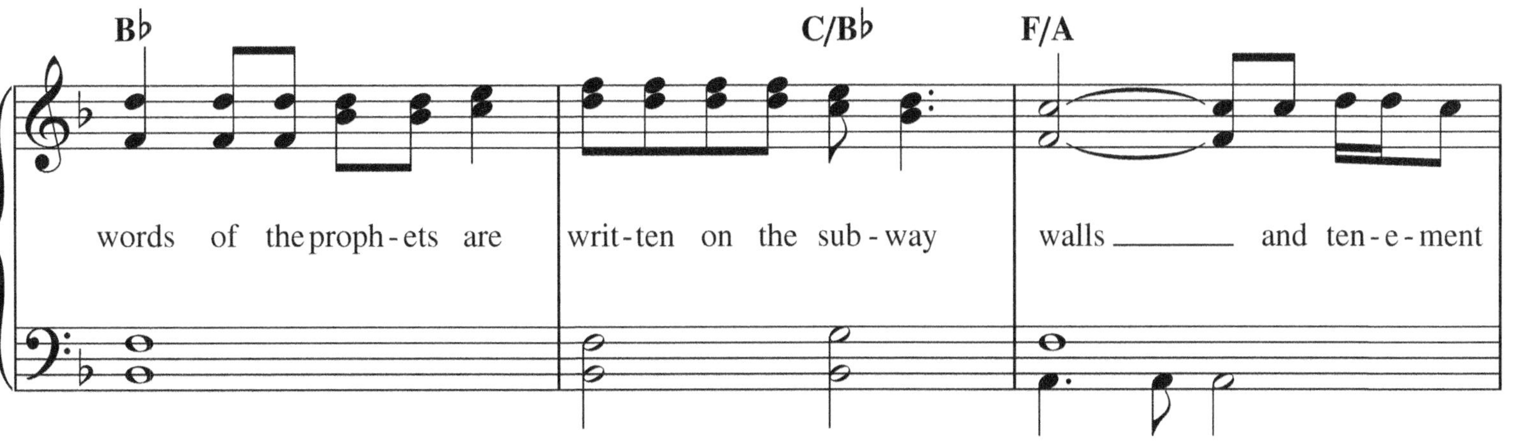
B♭
C/B♭
F/A
words of the proph - ets are
writ - ten on the sub - way
walls and ten - e - ment

Dm
F
C
halls, and
whis - per'd in the
sounds of

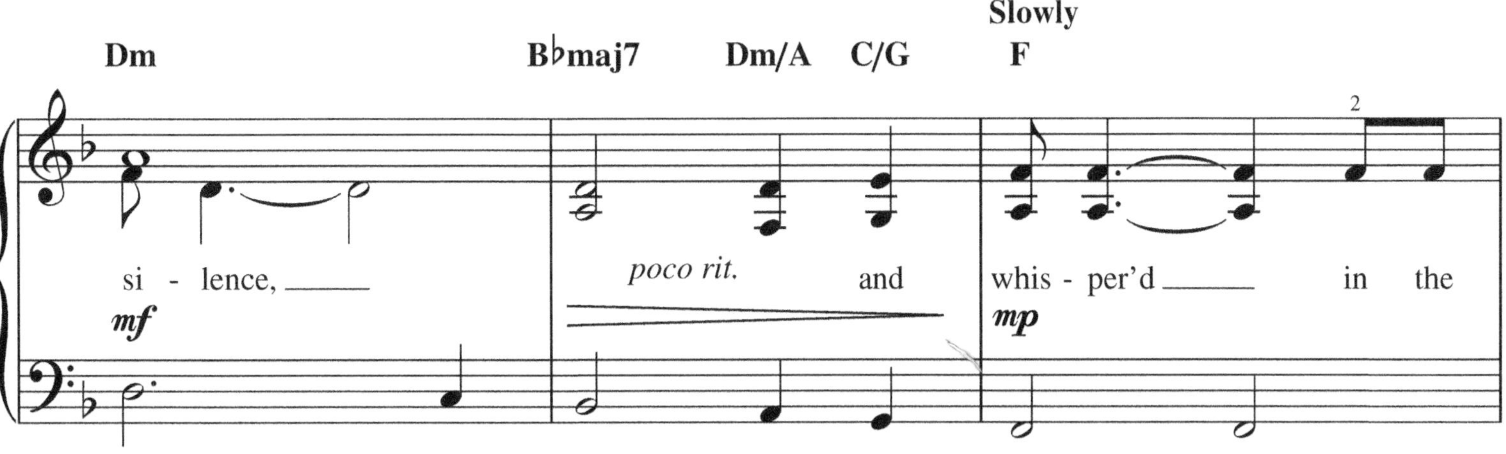
Dm
B♭maj7
Dm/A
C/G
Slowly
F
si - lence,
poco rit.
and
whis - per'd in the
mf
mp

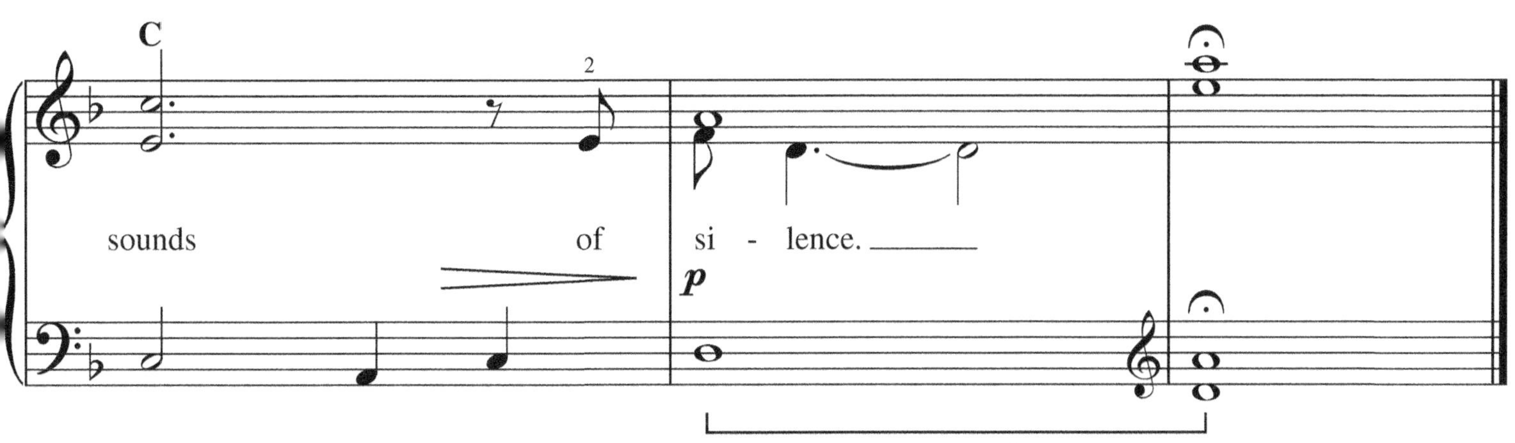
C
sounds of
si - lence.
p

STILL CRAZY AFTER ALL THESE YEARS

Words and Music by
PAUL SIMON

Cm7
F7
B♭
talked a - bout some old times and we drank our - selves some
ain't no fool for love songs that whis - per in my
Bdim
F/C
C7
Dm
beers.
ears.
Still cra - zy af - ter all these years;
Bdim7
F/C
C7
1.
B♭m7
oh, still cra - zy af - ter all these years.
C7
F
B♭/F
F/C
I'm not the

2.
F7
Cm7
F7
Gmaj7
years.
Four in the

D
Dm
F♯m7
morn - ing;
crapped out,
yawn - ing;
long - ing my

B7sus
B7
Emaj7
Dm7
life a -
way.
I'll nev - er

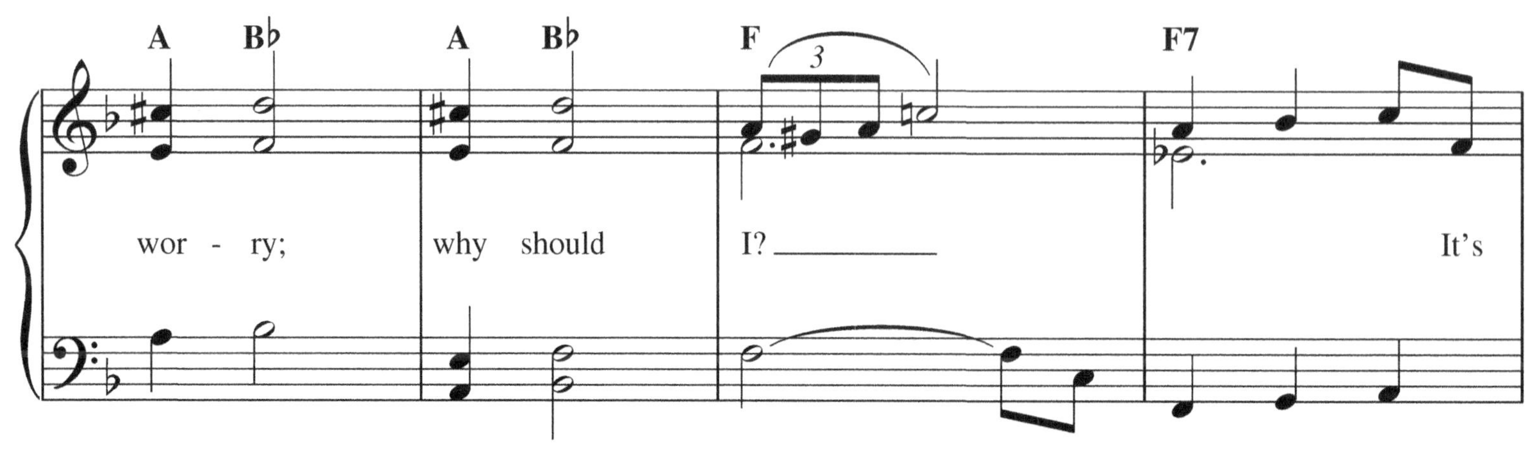
A
B♭
A
B♭
F
3
F7
wor - ry;
why should
I?
It's

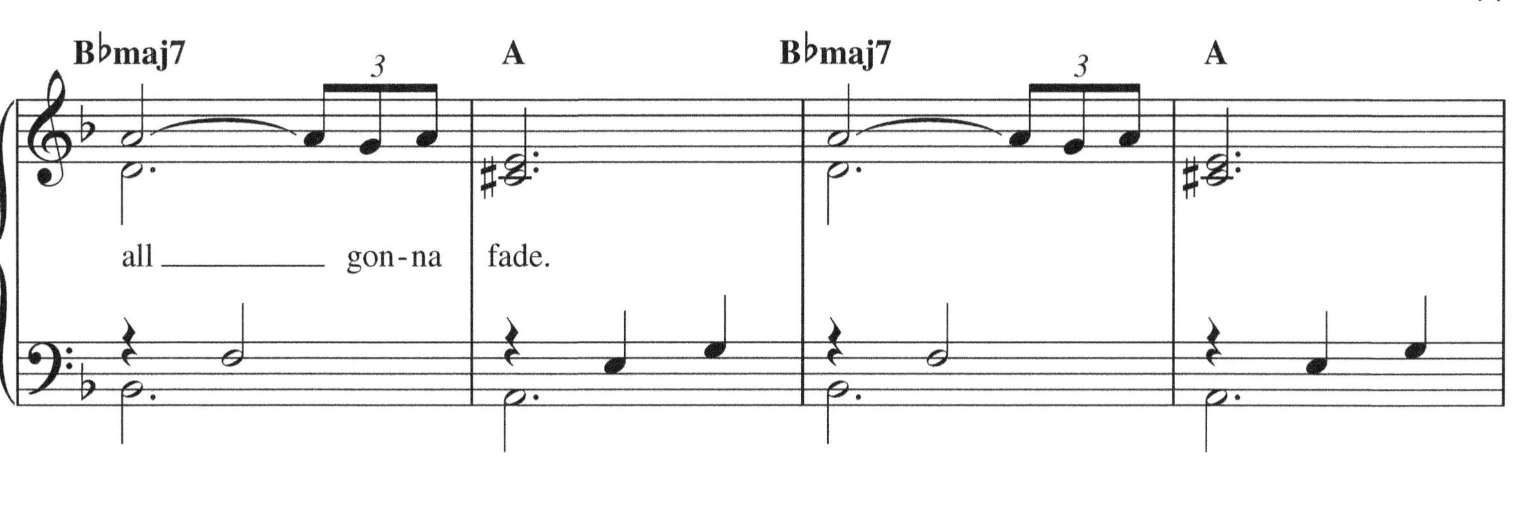
B♭maj7
3
A
B♭maj7
3
A
all gon-na fade.

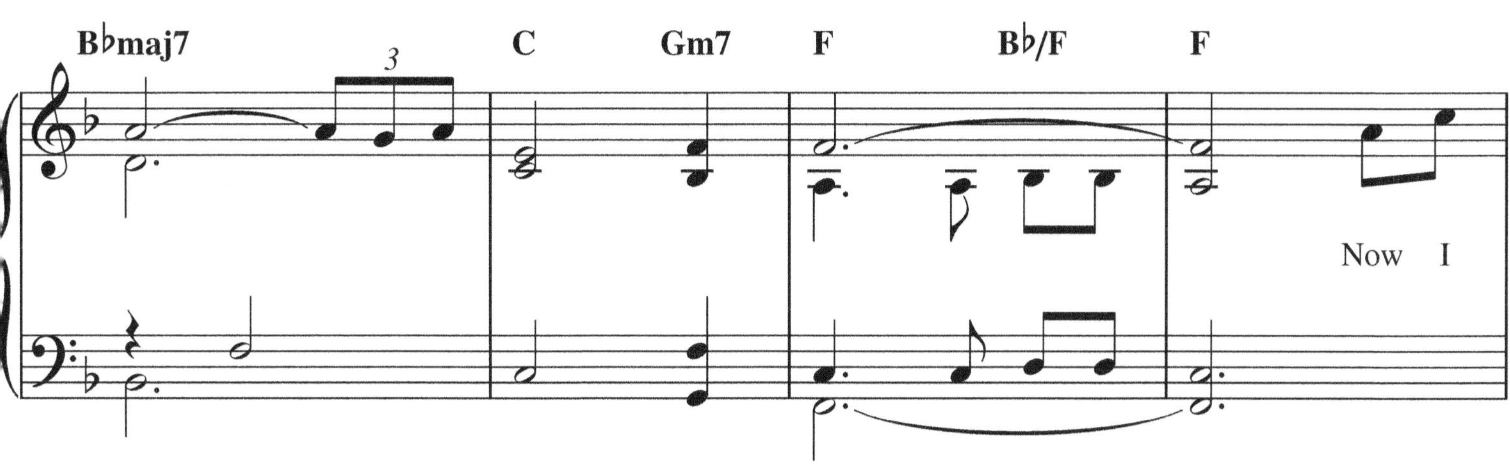
B♭maj7
3
C
Gm7
F
B♭/F
F
Now I

F7/A
B♭
E♭9
sit by my win-dow and I watch the cars; I

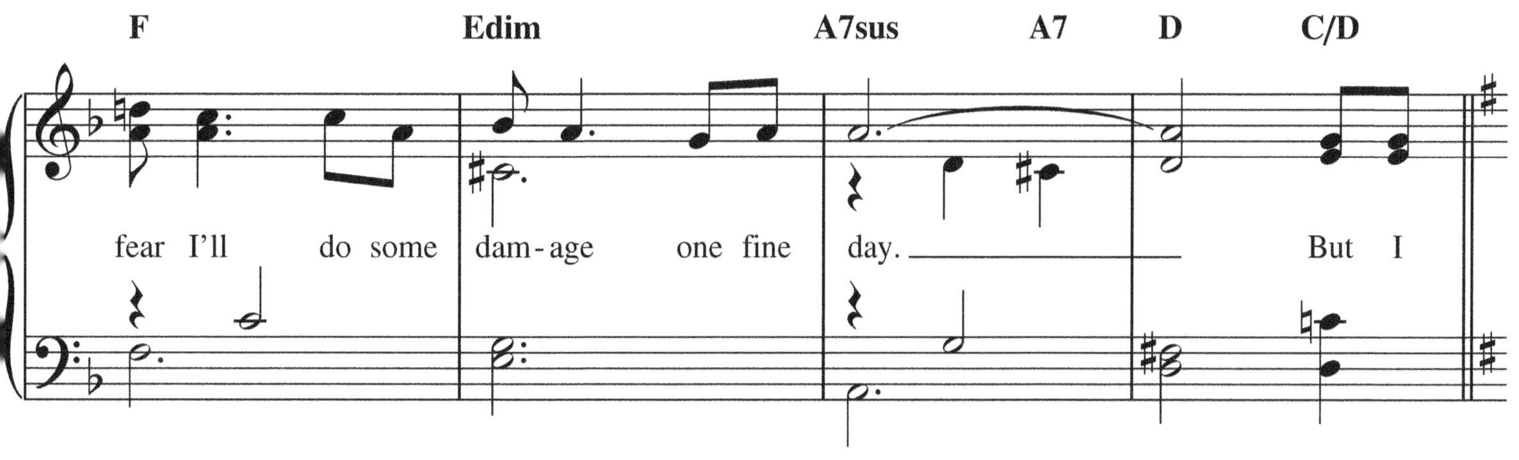
F
Edim
A7sus
A7
D
C/D
fear I'll do some dam-age one fine day. But I

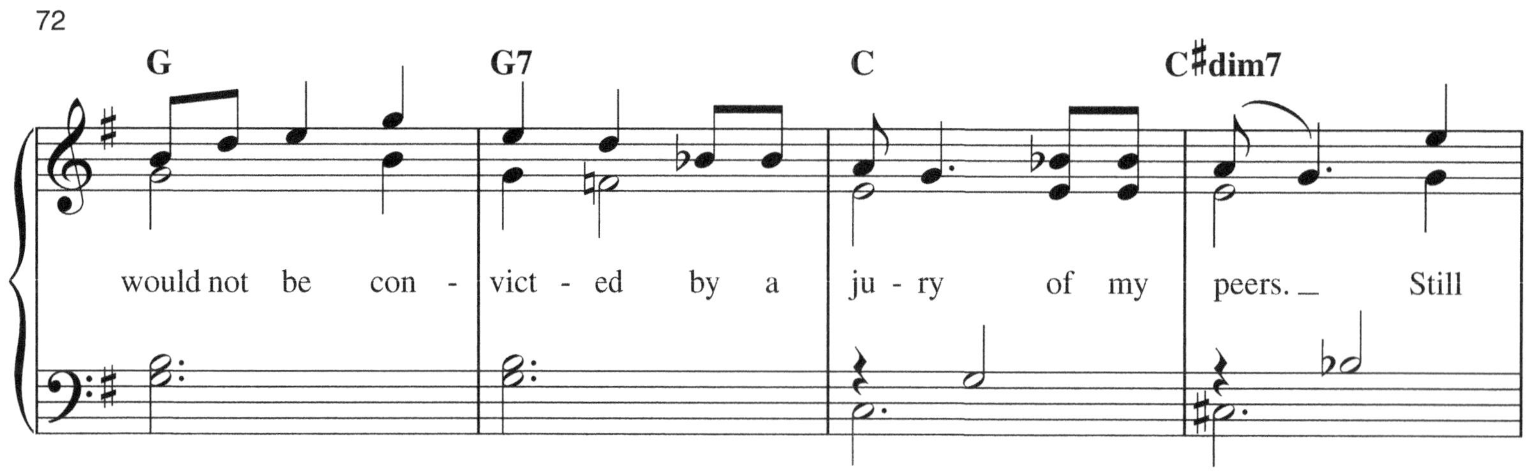
G
G7
C
C#dim7
would not be con - vict - ed by a ju - ry of my peers. Still

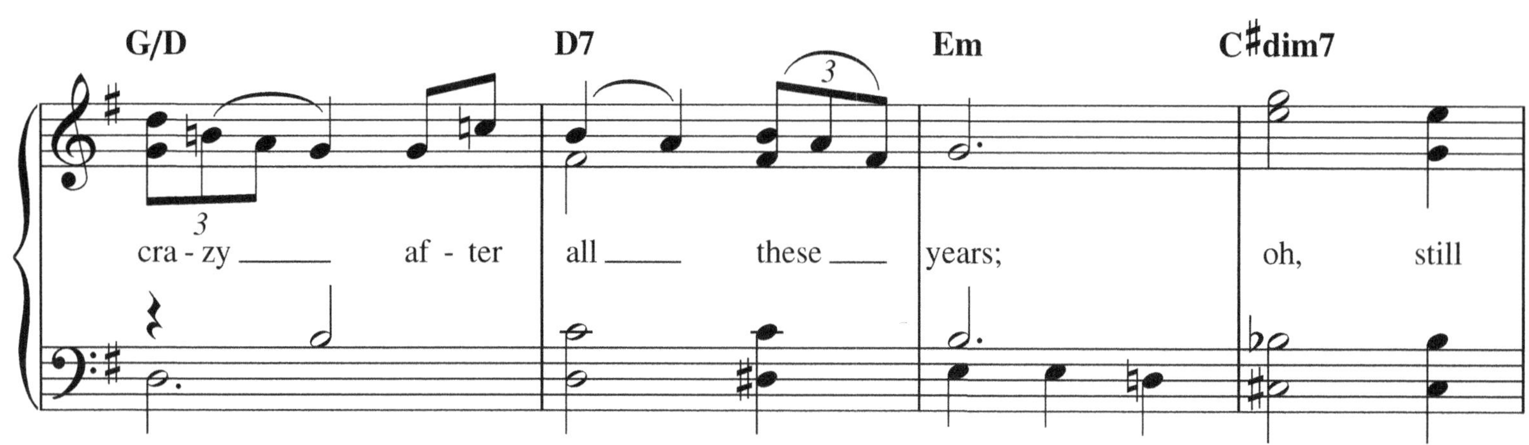
G/D
D7
Em
C#dim7
cra - zy after all these years; oh, still

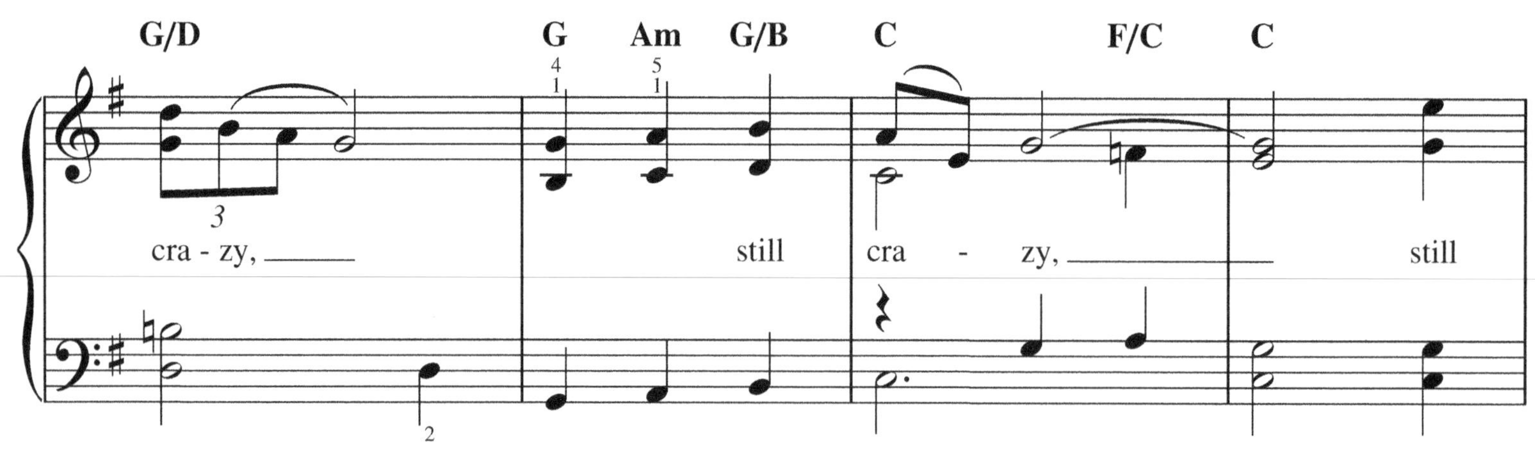
G/D
G Am G/B
C
F/C
C
cra - zy, still cra - zy, still

G/D
D7
G
C/G
G
cra - zy af - ter all these years.
rit.